MARVEL AGE OF COMICS

THE ULTIMATES

AN EXPLORATION BY

TED ADAMS

BLOOMSBURY ACADEMIC
NEW YORK · LONDON · OXFORD · NEW DELHI · SYDNEY

BLOOMSBURY ACADEMIC
Bloomsbury Publishing Inc, 1359 Broadway, New York, NY 10018, USA
Bloomsbury Publishing Plc, 50 Bedford Square, London, WC1B 3DP, UK
Bloomsbury Publishing Ireland, 29 Earlsfort Terrace, Dublin 2, D02 AY28, Ireland

BLOOMSBURY, BLOOMSBURY ACADEMIC and the Diana logo are
trademarks of Bloomsbury Publishing Plc

MARVEL PUBLISHING
Jeff Youngquist, VP, Production and Special Projects
Brian Overton, Manager, Special Projects
Sarah Singer, Editor, Special Projects
Jeremy West, Manager, Licensed Publishing
Sven Larsen, VP, Business Development and Licensed Publishing
David Gabriel, VP, Comic Sales and Content Planning
C.B. Cebulski, Editor-in-Chief

BLOOMSBURY ACADEMIC
Haaris Naqvi, Global Editorial Director
Leah Babb-Rosenfeld, Editorial Director
Hali Han, Assistant Editor
Ian Buck, Deputy Head of Production
Zeba Talkhani, Senior Production Editor
Ben Anslow, Senior Designer

First published in the United States of America 2026

© 2026 MARVEL

Cover art: Bryan Hitch, Paul Neary & Paul Mounts
Cover design: Ben Anslow

All rights reserved. No part of this publication may be: i) reproduced or transmitted in any form, electronic or mechanical, including photocopying, recording or by means of any information storage or retrieval system without prior permission in writing from the publishers; or ii) used or reproduced in any way for the training, development or operation of artificial intelligence (AI) technologies, including generative AI technologies. The rights holders expressly reserve this publication from the text and data mining exception as per Article 4(3) of the Digital Single Market Directive (EU) 2019/790.

Bloomsbury Publishing Inc does not have any control over, or responsibility for, any third-party websites referred to or in this book. All internet addresses given in this book were correct at the time of going to press. The author and publisher regret any inconvenience caused if addresses have changed or sites have ceased to exist, but can accept no responsibility for any such changes.

A catalog record for this book is available from the Library of Congress.

ISBN: PB: 979-8-7651-4164-9
ePDF: 979-8-7651-4166-3
eBook: 979-8-7651-4165-6

Series: Marvel Age of Comics

Typeset by RefineCatch Limited, www.refinecatch.com
Printed and bound the United States of America

For product safety related questions contact productsafety@bloomsbury.com.

To find out more visit www.bloomsbury.com/marvel-books

CONTENTS

1 Avengers Assemble! 1
2 The Road to the Ultimate Universe 9
3 Time for a Twenty-First-Century Reboot! 17
4 The Ultimates (Creative Team and Concept) Assemble! 33
5 The Ultimates—Super Human! 41
6 The Ultimates—Homeland Security! 71
7 Interlude: Ultimate Galactus 103
8 The Ultimates 2! 109
9 Where Are They Now? 131
10 The Ultimates Shape Pop Culture! 143

Notes 145
Acknowledgments 147
List of Illustrations 151
About the Author 155

1
Avengers Assemble!

When the Ultimate imprint was launched in 2000, it was intended to shake up the comic book world and give new readers a chance to join the fun. Marvel's creators were allowed to reboot Marvel's classic characters. Starting with *Ultimate Spider-Man* and *Ultimate X-Men*, the Ultimate line soon expanded to include *The Avengers* under the title *The Ultimates*. Writer Mark Millar and artist Bryan Hitch didn't just reboot *The Avengers*; they reimagined how super hero stories could be told for a twenty-first-century audience.

Releasing not long after the 9/11 terrorist attacks in 2001, *The Ultimates* were also a response to the new reality Americans faced. The super heroes in *The Ultimates* worked directly for the U.S. government. The U.S. President appeared, grounding the story in the real world. Millar's emphasis on sharp dialogue and characterization brought the characters to life, making them feel like real people—super heroes who made mistakes, and due to their powers, those mistakes could have dangerous and even fatal results.

Hitch's cinematic storytelling and effective use of double-page spreads and hyper-realistic detail made the comics feel like you were watching a movie. When these super heroes fight, Hitch shows the violence and resulting damage in detail.

All of these things made the comic books extremely successful. They were among the bestselling comic books of their era and continue to be available in collected editions for a modern audience.

The Avengers

Ant-Man: Wait! Before we separate, the Wasp and I have something to say! Each of us has a different power! If we combined forces, we could be almost unbeatable!

Iron Man: Work as a team? Why not? I'm for it!

Thor: There is much good we might do!

Hulk: I'm sick of bein' hunted and hounded! I'd rather be with you than against you! So, whether you like it or not, I'm joining the …

	the … Hey! What are you calling yourselves?
Wasp:	That's right! We need a name! It should be something colorful and dramatic like … The Avengers, or …
Ant-Man:	"Or" nothing! That's it! The Avengers!

The Avengers #1, September 1963

To fully appreciate *The Ultimates*, it's essential to revisit the series that laid the groundwork: *The Avengers*. Launched two years after *Fantastic Four*, *The Avengers* became Marvel's second super hero team book. The early issues by Stan Lee and Jack Kirby were pivotal, and it was these stories that Mark Millar and Bryan Hitch would reimagine for a twenty-first-century audience with *The Ultimates*. And in a virtuous circle, it's *The Ultimates* that would influence the first *Avengers* movie, where millions of people who weren't already comic book fans would be introduced to and entertained by Marvel's "Mightiest Super-Heroes!"

The Avengers #1 included no new characters but was rather a place where Lee and Kirby could tell more stories about the super heroes they were creating as part of the Marvel Age of Comics. Iron Man, Giant Man, Wasp, and Thor all had ongoing regular stories published on monthly or bi-monthly schedules. The other solo Marvel titles that were being published at the same time were co-created and drawn by Marvel's other

The Avengers assemble for the first time in *The Avengers* #1 (September 1963), cover by Jack Kirby and Dick Ayers.

powerhouse creator, Steve Ditko. So, Spider-Man and Doctor Strange likely weren't included because Kirby wouldn't have been as familiar with their stories, and that would have made it harder to keep the continuity straight. And, as we'll see, it was that continuity that was a big part of what made the Marvel Universe so compelling. In fact, the Fantastic Four make an appearance in *The Avengers* #1!

In the *Son of Origins of Marvel Comics*, Lee explained how he and Kirby put together the first Avengers team:

> As with all such projects, variety is one of the most necessary ingredients, so it was important to select a bevy of heroes who were all totally different. After kicking it around for a while, we came up with what seemed like a perfect combo. We'd start with the Hulk, just to make it difficult. Then, we'd include Thor, 'cause there's always room for a God of Thunder. Iron Man would be able to supply them all with weapons and bread whenever they needed it, and we'd toss in Ant-Man and the Wasp just for the sheer lunacy of it.

Captain America joins the team in *The Avengers* #4; Hawkeye, a reformed villain, joins in #16; and Black Widow, another reformed villain, becomes an ally to the team in #30.

The Marvel Universe

What Lee, Kirby, Ditko, and the other artists at Marvel did was create a universe where the continuity between comics was a regular part of the storytelling. If something happened in an issue of *Iron Man*, it could have an impact on a story in *The Avengers*, and characters would regularly cross over from one title to another.

This all started back in March 1963 when Spider-Man broke into the Fantastic Four's headquarters in *The Amazing Spider-Man* #1 and the Hulk fought the Fantastic Four in *Fantastic Four* #12. The early *Avengers* comics are full of cameos, with #3 featuring Spider-Man, the Fantastic Four, and the X-Men in a story that sees the team face off against both the Hulk and Sub-Mariner. That one issue showcases nearly every character in the Marvel Universe at the time. Fans loved it, and Marvel never looked back. Crossovers and stories that were built on top of other stories became the norm.

Marvel's shared universe would eventually have thousands of characters in it and storylines that recalled events that occurred in comics that were published decades before. By the 1970s, many comics were being written by the fans who'd grown up reading them, and they wanted to build on the stories they'd read and loved. So, by the 1990s, comic fans could be reading stories that were impacted by comic books that had been published before they were born. And it's important to remember that in the 1990s and early 2000s, not every Marvel comic was available to read digitally via Marvel Unlimited or through the comprehensive collections that are commonplace today.

The complicated chronology and continuity were part of what made comic books fun for the fans of the 1990s, but it also made it hard for new or casual readers to join the party. This era also saw comic book distribution move even more firmly away from the mainstream newsstands—which included grocery, drug, and convenience stores where everyone shopped—to comic book stores, which reached a much smaller audience.

In 1993, the popular "Maximum Carnage" storyline ran through fourteen Spider-Man comic books, and the reading order looked like this: *Spider-Man Unlimited* #1, *Web of Spider-Man* #101, *The Amazing Spider-Man* #378, *Spider-Man* #35, *The Spectacular Spider-Man* #201, *Web of Spider-Man* #102, *The Amazing Spider-Man* #379, *Spider-Man* #36, *Spectacular Spider-Man* #202, *Web of Spider-Man* #103, *Amazing Spider-Man* #380, *Spider-Man* #37, *The Spectacular Spider-Man* #203, and *Spider-Man Unlimited* #2.

Those are all fun comics, but they required a serious commitment from the reader and didn't allow for an easy entry point for a new reader who just wanted to read a comic book about Spider-Man. And as the '90s wore on, multi-title crossovers and stories that built on stories would become the norm.

So almost forty years after *Fantastic Four* #1's premiere in 1961, Marvel Comics would make the decision to create an entry point for new readers and introduce the Ultimate line and the title we're here to discuss, *The Ultimates* by Mark Millar and Bryan Hitch. Before we discuss *The Ultimates*, we'll first look at a low point in Marvel's history—the company's bankruptcy in 1996—and some of the wild publishing stunts that Marvel and other publishers were doing in that wild and wacky era. Marvel's emergence from bankruptcy and an industry-wide sales slump led the company to be more experimental than it had been in the past, and we'll check out the Marvel Knights imprint, a line of comic books that had an impact on the Ultimate line.

We'll examine all of that history and the other titles in the Ultimate line before discussing *The Ultimates*—and its sequel, *The Ultimates 2*—in detail. It's no exaggeration to say *The Ultimates* changed Marvel Comics forever and helped inspire the Marvel Cinematic Universe, which has become one of the biggest pop culture phenomena of all time.

But before we get there, let's take a time machine back to the Day-Glo days of the 1990s.

2
The Road to the Ultimate Universe

When the 1990s started, comic book sales were booming. *Spider-Man* #1 by Todd McFarlane sold more than two million copies in 1990 and was available with different covers that included gold, silver, and platinum versions and also came both poly-bagged and not poly-bagged. That huge number was shattered just a year later by Chris Claremont and Jim Lee with *X-Men* #1, which sold more than eight million copies and had four different covers that, when placed next to each other, made one large image. Claremont and Lee's sales record still stands today and is recognized by the Guinness World Records as the "best-selling comic, single edition."

This was a time when comic book publishers and retailers were benefitting from customers who were buying comic books as an investment. These speculators would buy multiple copies of the "hot" titles as if they were investing in the stock market.

To further entice these new customers, publishers tried new things that excited fans. In 1991, *The Incredible Hulk* #377 was printed with bright green Day-Glo inks and saw its sales skyrocket. Seeing how well that worked, *Silver Surfer* #50 was printed with the logo and the character embossed on the cover with a shiny silver foil, and *Ghost Rider* #15 showcased the character's flaming head printed with glow-in-the-dark ink.

Fan-focused magazines, like *Wizard* and *Hero Illustrated*, helped feed the frenzy by featuring monthly price guides and endless lists of the new "hot" comic books and creators. *Wizard*'s second issue was dated October 1991, and the "Top 10" hottest books were all Marvel titles, with *X-Men* #1 taking the top spot and *Spider-Man* #1 (platinum edition) coming in at the #6 spot.

Around the same time that *X-Men* #1 was hitting comic shops, Marvel Entertainment Group became a public company, under the ticker symbol MVL. The stock price almost immediately doubled, and the company's financial future looked golden. But some creative and business struggles, combined with an industry-wide decline in sales that saw 20% of comic book shops going out of business in 1993 alone, meant that the financial results weren't looking great for Marvel.[1] When things didn't improve, Marvel filed for bankruptcy in 1996.

But the type of bankruptcy Marvel filed didn't mean the company was going out of business; they were able to

The most '90s cover of them all, the Day-Glo *The Incredible Hulk* #377 (January 1991), cover by Dale Keown and Bob McLeod.

restructure their finances and keep publishing, even during this difficult period.

Before filing for bankruptcy in 1996, for the first time in its history, Marvel rebooted several of their characters in a storyline known as "Heroes Reborn." While it wasn't marketed as a separate imprint, this reimagining of core Marvel characters would act as a precedent for the Ultimate line.

The publishing plan saw Jim Lee and his WildStorm Productions studio taking on *Fantastic Four* and *Iron Man*, while Rob Liefeld and his Extreme Studios tackled *Captain America* and *The Avengers*. I was working for WildStorm when these comic books were created and remember the palpable excitement in the office when they were being worked on. Getting to see an early view of Jim's take on those classic Marvel characters is one of the highlights of my career.

This was also the era when collectible card games (CCGs) first became popular, and the team I managed at WildStorm was responsible for the WildStorms CCG. As the title implies, it focused on the characters in the WildStorm universe, but because of "Heroes Reborn," Marvel allowed us to include the Fantastic Four and Iron Man on some of our cards. For a lifelong Marvel fan like me, it was fun to be able to briefly work on their characters.

In the Liefeld-produced comics, the "Heroes Reborn" Avengers team was led by Captain America, with the other members including Thor, Vision, Scarlet Witch, Hellcat, Hawkeye, and Swordsman. Only a couple of these characters would overlap with *The Ultimates* lineup, but one plot point would be resurrected—in the "Heroes Reborn" reboot, Nick Fury and S.H.I.E.L.D. directed the actions of the team.

Sales were initially strong for the relaunched titles, but the experiment only lasted a year. By the time "Heroes Reborn" ended, sales for Marvel (and every other comic book publisher) were down significantly from the salad days of *X-Men* #1. The total number of comic books ordered in January 1990 was over ten million. By the end of 1999, sales had plummeted to almost half that number.[2]

Before the entire comic book industry started to contract, Joe Quesada and Jimmy Palmiotti, two popular comic book artists, started their own publishing company, Event Comics, in 1994. Before starting Event Comics, Quesada was a penciller who worked on a handful of titles for Valiant, DC, and Marvel. Palmiotti was an inker who worked on Marvel titles including *The Punisher*, *Ghost Rider*, and *Marvel Comics Presents*. They'd worked together on a number of comic book covers.

While Quesada and Palmiotti were getting Event off the ground, the characters from "Heroes Reborn" were returned to regular Marvel continuity with the aptly titled storyline "Heroes Return," and senior management at Marvel was looking to replicate the success they'd initially seen with those

Marvel's first family are rebooted for the first time in *Fantastic Four* #1 (November 1996), cover by Jim Lee and Scott Williams.

comics. The President of Marvel Comics, Joe Calamari, was impressed by what Quesada and Palmiotti were doing at Event and approached the pair in 1998 about overseeing a handful of titles—an imprint that would be known as Marvel Knights.

Quesada spoke about the state of the comic book industry during the period when he and Palmiotti were asked to start Marvel Knights:

> You have to frame it under the umbrella of what the comic book world was going through at this point: we were on the edge of extinction. And you really got that sense, or we really got that sense, from hanging out with people at Marvel. Because they were seeing the sales figures come in, and they weren't just watching sales drop. They were watching stores cease to exist, I mean like franchises. Gone. Hundreds and hundreds of stores closing, distributors closing.[3]

Like the deal Marvel did with Jim Lee and Rob Liefeld for "Heroes Reborn," Quesada and Palmiotti with Nanci Dakesian would handle all editorial responsibilities for the titles they were given. But instead of working remotely—both Lee and Liefeld produced their "Heroes Reborn" titles from their studios in California—the Marvel Knights team would have offices at Marvel's New York City headquarters, albeit on a different floor from the rest of the company.

The four titles in the Marvel Knights line were *Daredevil*,

Black Panther, *Inhumans*, and *Punisher*. Unlike the "Heroes Reborn" deal, they weren't given the company's premiere characters, and they weren't doing a reboot; the Marvel Knights stories would take place in Marvel's ongoing continuity. Marvel Knights was branded as an imprint within Marvel Comics, with the corner box on the cover clearly identifying the titles in the line.

Throughout the '90s, it was the artists who drove comic book sales for Marvel. The huge numbers for *Spider-Man* #1 and *X-Men* #1 were largely because of the art by Todd McFarlane and Jim Lee. When McFarlane and Lee formed Image Comics with other Marvel artists, their initial comics were equally focused on the art. When Marvel brought back Lee and Liefeld for "Heroes Reborn," it was with a similar art-forward aim.

It was Kevin Smith's run on the Marvel Knights *Daredevil* where that would start to change. The fan's attention would begin to shift towards the writer and the stories they were telling. This is a trend we'll continue to see when we discuss the Ultimate line. Smith's Daredevil stories, which combined darker plots with clever dialogue that often had pop culture references, would inspire the work Mark Millar would do on *The Ultimates*.

3
Time for a Twenty-First-Century Reboot!

In 2000, Bill Jemas, who had previously worked at the Marvel-owned trading card company Fleer, became Marvel's President of Publishing and New Media. The complicated comic book continuity that led Marvel to create the Heroes Reborn titles also frustrated Jemas and he wanted to try something new. Unlike many of the people who work in comic book publishing, Jemas didn't grow up reading and collecting comic books.

Jemas wanted to find a bigger audience, and that would mean finding new readers. If that meant alienating some fans, he could live with it. It was time to attempt what had been, up until then, the unthinkable—rebooting Marvel's most popular characters, Spider-Man and the X-Men.

A February 2000 announcement from Marvel said:

> Loyal comic fans have earned an inside knowledge and insight through five, ten or twenty years of reading. The Marvel Universe is the longest-running continuous story in history, and it's very difficult, in that context, to do anything new that's not tied to that continuity. Lose the continuity, and you lose your most important customers.

It went on to say:

> Marvel believes that the *Ultimate Spider-Man* and *X-Men* lines are the answer! Core comic fans will love these books. The characters are pure and true to themselves. The stories are strong, complete, compelling and produced by our best artists and writers. But any new reader can pick up any of these books and start reading. Essentially, the Ultimates swap out the traditional backstory and replace it with a rich, self-contained, year-2000 context.

It continued, practically yelling at the reader, "THE ULTIMATES [IMPRINT] WILL BE MARKETED TO NEW READERS."

Jemas, of course, couldn't afford to just stop publishing all of the titles in the regular Marvel Universe, so those would all continue, and Marvel would essentially have two separate continuities running. The Ultimate line would have a teenage

Spider-Man, and the regular Marvel Universe would have a thirty-something one.

Jemas also wanted a new editor-in-chief. He was impressed by Joe Quesada, telling *Wizard*: "Marvel Knights was making the best comic books in the business—the best looking, the best written. They were reader-friendly and commercially viable." So, he offered Quesada the Editor-in-Chief job at Marvel, and he took it.

Jemas and Quesada knew what they wanted to do; now they just needed to find creators who could make it happen.

Ultimate Spider-Man Creative Team

Brian Michael Bendis

Brian Michael Bendis, who would become one of the most successful comic book writers of all time, started his career as a writer and artist. His first work was with the small comic book publisher Caliber Press, where he published *Parts of a Hole* (1991), *Quivers* (1991), and *Fire* (1993).

While Bendis was building his career, Bill Jemas wrote a plot for the first six issues of the rebooted Spider-Man and set out to find a writer. In the August 2000 issue, Jemas told *Wizard* what he liked about Bendis: "[He] does some of the best, fastest, hottest dialogue in the business. And he's got a real sense of modern-day society."

Bendis saw his job as

> … a relaunching of Spider-Man as Stan Lee envisioned him, but written as dramatically and entertainingly as possible, as if the events that shaped the young Peter Parker started today. There is nothing we are doing to Spider-Man that isn't in the spirit of the theme and characters that were originally invented. The only thing we are doing is freeing the characters from 40 looooong years of sometimes four-Spidey-titles-a-month continuity.[4]

Mark Bagley

While Bendis was a well-regarded writer when he got the *Ultimate Spider-Man* job, it was his first work for Marvel Comics. Joining the Marvel rookie on art would be a veteran Marvel artist who first started working for the company in 1987.

Over the next few years, Mark Bagley would work on a number of Marvel titles before getting assigned as the regular artist on *The Amazing Spider-Man*, starting with #351 (1991). He would stay on the title for five years.

Bagley explains how he got the *Ultimate Spider-Man* job:

Bill Jemas really wanted me on this. He's really involved with Brian on the storytelling. He feels like it's his baby. Apparently, he was very involved in the Spider-Man trading card series that I did several years ago, and apparently became a really big fan of my stuff. I was the guy he wanted to have this book. And hey, who am I to say no to the president of the company?[5]

Art Thibert

Art Thibert's first work for Marvel was a short run on Marvel UK's *Transformers* comic, where he worked on the back-up stories featuring The Inhumanoids. Thibert started getting regular work from both DC and Marvel on premiere titles like *Action Comics* (featuring Superman) and *The Uncanny X-Men*. In the mid-'90s, he mostly worked for Image Comics, where he created *Black & White*, a three-issue series that he wrote and drew.

In 1996, Thibert returned to Marvel, where he mostly worked on X-Men-related titles, including *The Uncanny X-Men*. A prolific inker with a long track record of reliability, Thibert was chosen to work on both *Ultimate Spider-Man* and *Ultimate X-Men*.

Ultimate Spider-Man

In *Amazing Fantasy* #15, Stan Lee and Steve Ditko may have told the best super hero origin story of all time. In an eleven-page story, Peter Parker is established as a high school science nerd who is bullied by classmates, gets bitten by the radioactive spider that gives him his powers, makes his own costume and web-shooters, tries to make money with his new powers, fails to stop the bad guy who then kills his uncle, and ends the story by accepting that "with great power there must also come great responsibility." These plot elements are the engine that would drive thousands of stories. So, long-time Marvel fans were initially skeptical about the idea of rebooting one of their favorite characters and his perfect origin story, particularly when it was written by a writer unknown to many of them.

The first issue of *Ultimate Spider-Man* was double-sized, having forty-eight pages, and the title page included a caption box that read "Based on the original story in *Amazing Fantasy* #15 by Stan Lee and Steve Ditko." It also gave a shared "story" credit to Bill Jemas. The other members of the creative team were Steve Buccellato, colorist; and Richard Starkings and Comicraft, letterer.

That extra-sized first issue sets a slower pace for the series, with the only plot points that get established from *Amazing Fantasy* #15 being that Peter Parker is a high school science nerd who is seriously bullied by his fellow classmates (and gym teacher!), the spider bite, and the realization the bite has given him powers. The issue ends with Peter discovering he can stick to the wall in a nice splash page that shows him upside down on the ceiling saying, "Whoa—cool."

The slower pace doesn't mean the issue isn't entertaining. Bendis does a nice job of blending in elements of the Spider-Man story that happened long after *Amazing Fantasy* #15. The best example is Norman Osborn owns the lab where Peter gets bitten by the spider. Long-time Spider-Man fans will recognize Norman Osborn as the real name of the Green Goblin. It also allows Bendis and Bagley to more fully develop the characters, particularly the relationship between Peter and his aunt and uncle. It's a good story that boded well for the start-up Ultimate line.

Comic book stores were willing to take a gamble on the reboot, and *Ultimate Spider-Man* #1 placed #15 on the list of the top-selling comic books of September 2000. That was better than the regular version of the character, with *The Amazing Spider-Man* issue that came out that month placing #18 on the list and *Peter Parker: Spider-Man* coming in at #23.

But the goal of the Ultimate line was to reach new readers, so sales in comic book stores, which were likely only selling to Marvel's existing readers, weren't the point. To reach new readers, Marvel arranged for *Ultimate Spider-Man* #1 to be sold and given away at Wal-Mart, Target, KB Toys, and, oddly, in Buster Brown shoe boxes sold at Payless Shoes. The number distributed was never fully disclosed but has been estimated at eight million copies.[6] Giving away all those free copies must have worked, because by #16, Marvel reported (for Postal Service reasons) paid sales of 354,115. Mission accomplished for the *Ultimate Spider-Man*—more people were reading Spider-Man, and, presumably, most of them were new readers.

And that was just the start. As planned, the first *Ultimate Spider-Man* collected edition, which collected the first seven issues, came out only one month after #7. The relatively slow pace of the storytelling worked well when the entire story was read as one volume and not just as chapters that came out once a month. Unlike comic books published today, where almost every series or storyline is eventually collected into a trade paperback, that was not the case with every comic book published in 2000. This meant it hadn't yet become commonplace for writers and artists to pace their stories for the collected edition. The success of *Ultimate Spider-Man* Vol. 1—it was the second-bestselling graphic novel of 2001 in comic book stores and the top-selling graphic novel at Barnes & Noble—would encourage other creators to take a slower approach to their storytelling.

The fan response was positive, with the creators and title

winning a number of awards in the 2001 Wizard Fan Awards. Contemporary critics also liked the series. Marvel ran an ad that had four glowing pull quotes, including this one from Randy Lander of Comics Newsarama: "This is a reflection of what Spidey would look like if created today instead of the 1960s and it's even better than my expectations … it works."

Also in 2002, the first "Free Comic Book Day" was held to coincide with the opening of the first *Spider-Man* movie. Held once a year, Free Comic Book Day encourages new customers to visit a comic book store for free comic books. Not surprisingly, the comic book Marvel chose for retailers to give away was a reprint of *Ultimate Spider-Man* #1, expanding even further the audience for the Ultimate line.

Ultimate Spider-Man would run for 133 issues, with Bendis and Bagley working together for the first 110 issues, setting the record for the longest-running creative team on a Marvel comic book (beating Stan Lee and Jack Kirby's record of 102 issues of *Fantastic Four*).

Bendis also wrote all sixteen issues of *Ultimate Marvel Team-Up*, the third Ultimate series (releasing after *Ultimate X-Men*). *Ultimate Marvel Team-Up* was an homage to the long-running Marvel title of the same name that originally appeared in 1972 and ran for 150 issues. They both featured Spider-Man teaming up with other Marvel heroes. In the Ultimate version, most of the characters Spider-Man meets are making their first appearance as Ultimate characters, including, as we'll soon see, some of *The Ultimates* heroes.

Ultimate X-Men Creative Team

Mark Millar

Brian Michael Bendis was originally announced as the writer of *Ultimate X-Men*. When he pivoted to focus on his Spider-Man titles, *Ultimate X-Men* ended up in the very capable hands of Mark Millar. Like Bendis, Millar would become one of the most successful comic book writers of all time.

Millar, born in Scotland, got his first comic book published in 1991 with a short-lived UK publisher. It told the story of a super hero who was either the second coming of Jesus Christ or the antichrist, quickly establishing Millar as a writer who didn't mind courting controversy. That series brought him to the attention of the editorial team responsible for a long-running UK science fiction anthology. From there, it wasn't long before he was writing super hero comics for U.S. publishers.

Adam Kubert

For Adam Kubert and his brother, Andy, drawing comic books is the family business. Their dad, Joe Kubert, had his first comic

The all-new Spider-Man. This title's success would allow Marvel to expand the Ultimate line. *Ultimate Spider-Man* #1 (November 2000), cover by Joe Quesada.

book art published in 1942 and is one of the most prolific comic book artists of all time.

Adam started working regularly for Marvel, beginning with *Ghost Rider & Blaze: Spirits of Vengeance*, where he penciled twelve of the first thirteen issues. He then moved to Marvel's popular *Wolverine* title, which he would draw from 1993 to 1996. Having proven to be both reliable and a fan favorite, Kubert was given Marvel's top-selling title, *The Uncanny X-Men*.

So, Adam Kubert was already drawing the X-Men when he took on the *Ultimate X-Men* assignment. He told *Wizard*, in their September 2000 issue, "It's a chance to work on something and build from the ground up. Who wouldn't want that opportunity?"

Ultimate X-Men

Miller agreed with the concept of the Ultimate line, telling *Wizard* in their December 2002 issue: "I found Marvel's complex history and three-and-a-half thousand super characters daunting. Starting from scratch gave me and Brian [Michael Bendis] the same excitement there must have been in 1962. There was no feeling of restraint when putting this together." Joining Millar, Kubert, and Thibert were colorist Richard Isanove and letterers Richard Starkings and Wes Abbott.

When Marvel published the *X-Men* #1 (by Stan Lee, Jack Kirby, and Paul Reinman) in September 1963, the reader was thrown right into the story. Like the origin story of Spider-Man in *Amazing Fantasy* #15, almost all the elements that would drive thousands of X-Men stories were put into place in their first issue.

On the very first page of that first issue, the X-Men characters already had their costumes and code names (Angel, Beast, Cyclops, and Iceman). The story starts with the four X-Men training, a scene that allows the reader to learn more about each character and their individual powers. X-Men training in their Danger Room (which got its name in *X-Men* #2) is a regular occurrence in almost every iteration of the X-Men. There's even a story arc where the Danger Room gains consciousness and a humanoid form.

We also meet the wheelchair-bound Professor X and Jean Grey, who is just arriving at the school. Professor X tells her, "You, Miss Grey, like the other four students at this most exclusive school, are a mutant! You possess an extra power … one which ordinary humans do not!! That is why I call my students … X-Men, for ex-tra power!" Professor X also explains that it's the job of the X-Men to stop evil mutants from harming humans, and, to that effect, they battle Magneto. He is, of course, the villain, and occasional ally, that would be their main nemesis through many iterations of the characters.

There is one plot point in the first issue that will change dramatically over time. The battle with Magneto takes place at a base defended by the U.S. military. After they defeat Magneto, the base's commander thanks the team and says, "I promise you that before this day is over, the X-Men will be the most honored in my command." It doesn't take long before Homo sapiens begin to fear mutants, and many X-Men storylines are driven by that conflict.

Fear of mutants is what starts the story in *Ultimate X-Men* #1. We witness the giant Sentinel androids soaring into Los Angeles, where they kill several mutants. One of the Sentinels even goes so far as to crush a mutant beneath its robotic foot, producing a loud "crunch" sound effect, accompanied by the remnants of bone and lots of blood. This is in response to a bomb the Brotherhood of Mutants, led by Magneto, set off in Washington D.C. As we'll soon see, that bomb will also set in motion the creation of the Ultimates.

The rest of *Ultimate X-Men* #1 follows Jean Grey as she recruits three new students to join The Xavier Institute for Gifted Children. The team wears "black latex uniforms" that are similar to the ones found in the 2000 *X-Men* movie. Not only does this make the characters more recognizable to the new audience that the Ultimate line is designed to attract, but we're also told they cloak the wearer from the mutant-hunting Sentinels. It's revealed at the end of the issue that the fan-favorite character Wolverine is about to join the story.

So, with the first three Ultimate titles successfully established, it was time for Marvel to turn its attention to the title that would have the biggest impact on the company's pop culture dominance, the Ultimate version of *The Avengers—The Ultimates*. And fans were ready for it. When asked in an online survey by *Wizard* in their November 2002 issue "What Marvel character should get the 'Ultimate' treatment," 36% said The Avengers, Hulk got 18% of the vote, and Captain America got 15%.

The first roll call of the newly formed Ultimate X-Men. *Ultimate X-Men* #1 (February 2001), story by Mark Millar, art by Adam Kubert and Art Thibert.

4

The Ultimates (Creative Team and Concept) Assemble!

You might be wondering why *The Ultimates* wasn't called *Ultimate Avengers* like the Spider-Man and X-Men titles that preceded it. Millar told *Entertainment Weekly* that it was because the regular Avengers comic books weren't popular at the time.[7] In the month the first issue of *The Ultimates* was released, the bestselling *Avengers* comic book was an issue from the eight-issue mini-series *The Avengers: Celestial Quest*. It only sold around 30,000 copies.

A review published in 2002 thought *The Ultimates* name was "dumb" but went on to say:

I might buy the government choosing the name for its presumed appeal to young Americans, a subliminal "recruitment" plan for additional super-soldier squads. A writer could [w]ring an intriguing scenario from a government campaign urging youngsters to "be the ultimate you can be" and showing what happens to a teenager who enlists in the program.[8]

Even though they didn't use the name, the initial line-up of the team is almost entirely the same as the one found in those early *Avengers* comic books—Iron Man, Giant Man, the Wasp, Captain America, and Thor. The biggest difference is that the Ultimates work for the U.S. government, under the direction of Nick Fury.

With the title and team members settled, Millar described his approach to the characters that would make up the team to *Wizard* in their September 2002 issue: "*The Ultimates* is another step in the direction these kinds of characters have been taking for thousands of years. They started off as gods and have been working their way down to the streets for centuries. *The Ultimates* is very much an old-fashioned Marvel book—realistic heroes with problems being the root of the success achieved by 1960s Marvel."

The series would loosely spin out of a storyline in *Ultimate X-Men* where Magneto attacked Washington D.C. That attack spurs the U.S. federal government to give Nick Fury and S.H.I.E.L.D. billions of dollars to form a group of "ultra-humans" as insurance against future super-powered disasters.

As we will see, like *The Avengers* versions before them, these characters have flaws, and, in some cases, very serious ones. Talking about their flaws—and foreshadowing some of what we'll discuss—Millar said:

> The flaws have certainly changed because they reflect the modern world, but heroism is a very simple concept that has changed very little since the dawn of man. The very concept of heroism is doing something to help other people even if it puts your own life in danger. That works as well in *The Ultimates* as it did in Greek myths. The foibles are interesting though and, yes, I suppose we pushed these to the limit in [*The*] *Ultimates*, but I don't think we compromised the characters in doing so. Tony was always a drinker, Hank had a history of domestic violence, Banner was always consumed by self-loathing. We just applied modern storytelling techniques, but they're essentially the same characters.[9]

Bryan Hitch

Like Millar, Bryan Hitch is a UK citizen. His first work was for Marvel's UK division on *Action Force*. Essentially a UK version of *G.I. Joe*, Hitch's first work appeared in *Action Force* #35, an issue written by Richard Starkings, who would go on to become one of the best-known comic book letterers of all time. He worked on that series for another eight issues—only providing covers for two of the issues—and other Marvel UK titles, including *The Transformers*, *Doctor Who Magazine*, *ThunderCats*, and *Death's Head*. Hitch made the transition to the mother ship, Marvel Comics, with *The Sensational She-Hulk* #9, written again by Richard Starkings (and Gregory Wright).

Andrew Currie

Andrew Currie, like Millar and Hitch, is also a British-born artist. Which means the writer and artists of this very American title, about a team of super heroes who work for the U.S. government, were all from the UK.

Currie quickly got work from Marvel, penciling the eight-issue *Super Soldiers* series from the Marvel Comics UK imprint, which is not the same as Marvel UK, where Hitch got his start. The distinction is that Marvel UK titles were only offered for sale in the UK, whereas Marvel Comics UK was an imprint published by Marvel Comics, and, therefore, those titles were available anyplace Marvel Comics were sold.

While working on *Super Soldiers*, Currie also penciled a few issues of *Avengers West Coast* and a *Punisher Annual*.

Paul Mounts

Paul Mounts got his start as a colorist with Marvel in 1989 on *Arena*, a graphic novel written and drawn by Bruce Jones, and *The Sensational She-Hulk in Ceremony*, a two-issue comic book series written by Dwyane McDuffie and Robin D. Chaplik, with art provided by June Brigman and Stan Drake.

By the time he took on the coloring job for *The Ultimates* in 2002, Mounts had worked on hundreds of comic books, including everything from *The Ren & Stimpy Show*, which surprisingly ran for forty-four issues, to *X-Men: Children of the Atom*, a six-issue series written by Joe Casey, with art by Steve Rude, Paul Smith, and Esad Ribic.

Mounts employs a subtle color palette in *The Ultimates*, which complements Hitch and Currie's artwork and enhances the realistic portrayal of the characters.

Chris Eliopoulos

Like Mounts, Chris Eliopoulos was a long-time veteran of the comic book industry by the time he lettered *The Ultimates*. His first work appears to be in 1990, operating as part of a group of letterers credited as "all available," on *The Uncanny X-Men* #257, written by Chris Claremont, with art by Jim Lee and Josef Rubinstein.

Also, like Mounts, Eliopoulos worked on an eclectic list of titles for Marvel, including *Barbie Fashion*, *NFL SuperPro Special Edition*, and *Men in Black: Retribution*, and lots of super hero titles, including *X-Force*, *Mutant X*, and *X-Men: The Movie*.

Comic book lettering is traditionally done with all upper-case letters. *Ultimate Spider-Man*, *Ultimate X-Men*, and *Ultimate Marvel Team-Up* were all initially lettered this way. However, *The Ultimates* broke from tradition by using both upper- and lower-case letters. This choice may have been made to resemble prose fiction more closely. Whatever the reason, the use of mixed-case lettering worked well for *The Ultimates*, reinforcing its more serious take on super heroes.

Ralph Macchio

Ralph Macchio, editor for all of the early Ultimate titles (he took over *Ultimate X-Men* from Mark Powers with #15), got his start in the comic book business in 1977 as one of the five writers who contributed to *Fantastic Four* #183 (only Bill Mantlo got a credit in the book). His first credited work as a writer was in *Spidey Super Stori*es #24. The version of Spider-Man in that series was inspired by the character's appearance on the children's TV show, *The Electric Company*. Fun fact: Spider-Man's appearance on that show marked the first time the character was portrayed as a live-action person on film. Macchio did one more issue of *Spidey Super Stories* before becoming the regular writer for *Marvel Two-in-One*, a series that teamed up The Thing from Fantastic Four with other Marvel characters. Other notable writing credits include the adaptation of David Lynch's *Dune* movie, the first issue of *The Transformers*, *X-Men Adventures*, and an adaptation of the 2000 *X-Men* movie.

Like many writers at Marvel, Macchio also served as an editor for the company, where he worked on titles that included *Master of Kung Fu*, *Rom*, and *Micronauts*. From the mid-'80s to mid-'90s, he was the editor for many years of *Thor*, *Captain America*, and *The Avengers*—all of which would serve him well as the editor of *The Ultimates*. Before starting on the Ultimate line, Macchio had been working on the Spider-Man line of books.

With the creative team now in place, the Ultimates are ready to assemble.

5

The Ultimates—Super Human!

Issue 1: Super Human

Millar said his work on *The Ultimates* was going to be unlike anything he'd done before, he wasn't kidding. It's unlike any other first issue of a super hero team book. Because it's not a team book at all—it's a Captain America World War II story.

Captain America first appeared in the Golden Age of comics when a wave of super heroes flooded newsstands after DC's *Action Comics* #1, featuring Superman, was bought by millions of kids across the United States. Created by Joe Simon and Jack Kirby, *Captain America Comics* #1 was published by Timely Publications, the predecessor to Marvel, and released in December 1940 with a March 1941 cover date. It featured a cover with Captain America punching Hitler, a full year before the U.S. entered World War II.

In it, Steve Rogers wants to join the army but is rejected

because of his scrawny body. He volunteers to be injected with a "strange seething liquid" that turns him into what is planned to be "the first of a corps of super-agents whose mental and physical ability will make them a terror to spies and saboteurs!" Steve is dubbed Captain America by the scientist who transformed him, but before more super-agents can be made, Nazi spies crash into the lab, killing the scientist and blowing up his equipment.

Captain America Comics was wildly successful during World War II, selling as many as a million copies per issue, but by the time the last issue came out in 1950, kids had mostly lost interest in super heroes and were reading comics about funny animals, cowboys, teenagers in love, and criminals. The last two issues of *Captain America Comics* even saw the title changed to *Captain America's Weird Tales,* and the last issue, #75, didn't even have a Captain America story in it. All the stories in that issue were horror ones, designed to cash in on that current fad.

It would be more than twenty years before Captain America would return to newsstands in *The Avengers* #4, which came out in January 1964 in a story written by Stan Lee and drawn by Jack Kirby. In that story, which took place right at the beginning of what would become known as the Marvel Universe, Stan Lee declared Captain America's return would be "A Tale Destined To Become A Magnificent Milestone In The Marvel Age Of Comics!"

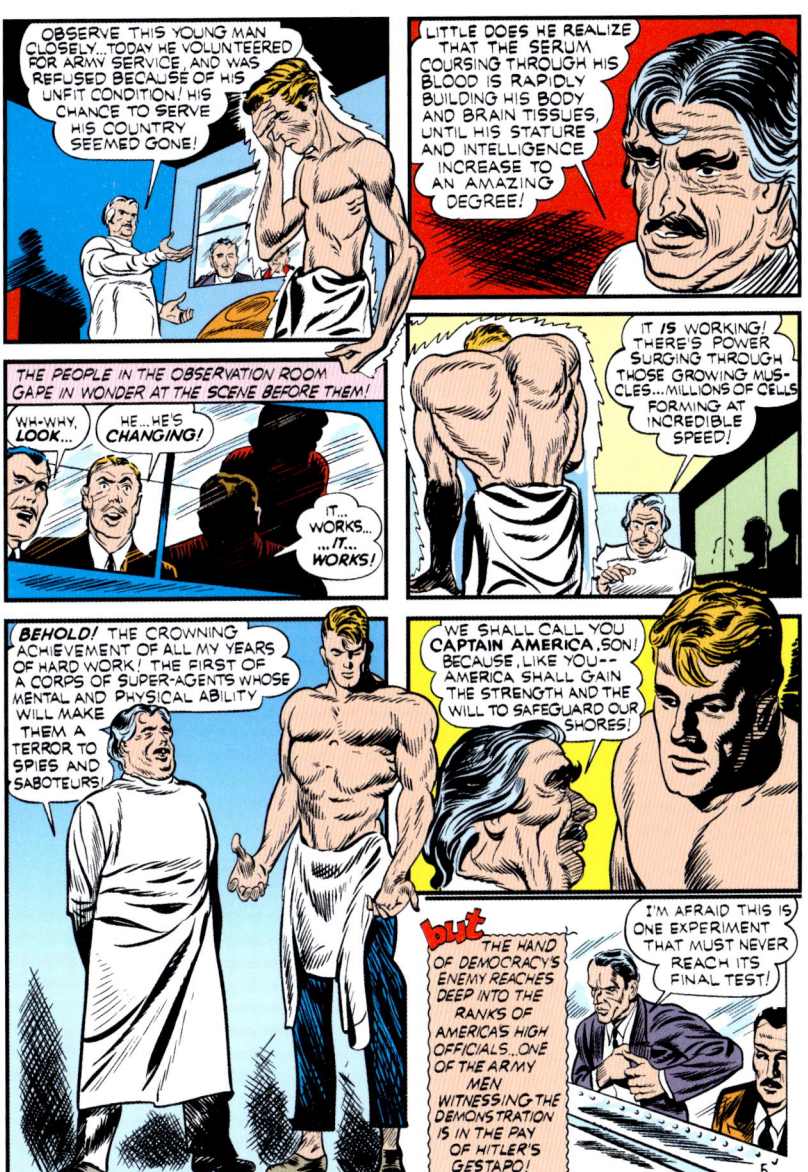

The original Captain America transforms after receiving an injection of a "strange seething liquid." *Captain America Comics* #1 (March 1941), story and art by Joe Simon and Jack Kirby.

The Avengers members in *The Avengers* #4 were Iron Man, Giant Man, Thor, and Wasp—the same characters that appear in *The Ultimates*—and the story starts with Sub-Mariner, the misunderstood "monarch of the sea," escaping from a battle with our heroes. He stops in the North Sea and encounters a group of "accursed humans" who are genuflecting in front of a frozen block of ice that contains a human-shaped form. In a fit of anger, Sub-Mariner throws the block of ice into the sea and storms off.

The Avengers, who are searching for Sub-Mariner, come across the ice block and bring it aboard their ship only to discover that, of course, it's a rapidly thawing Captain America. Cap quickly recovers and proves he still has his mettle by taking on and beating the entire Avengers team. It's not long before Steve Rogers is the leader of the team, a position he or someone else using the Captain America name would often maintain all the way to today.

About the Ultimate version of Captain America. Millar told *Wizard* in their October 2001 issue:

> I see Cap more along the lines of a cool, buzz-cut John Glenn kind of guy with an authority second only to the President himself in terms of commanding the United States Army and Navy. He knows what it's like to be crawling along Omaha Beach with his pals' guts splattered all over

his face. Cap should be a fairly haunted man, but somebody we can always count on to save our asses no matter what the odds.

Hitch also does a nice job with the character design—Captain America wears a helmet with a chin strap, modified flight goggles, and a tunic with a star on his chest. We only briefly see his shield, but it has the triangle shape that was used in the 1940s comic books. A similar costume and shield were used in part of 2011's *Captain America: The First Avenger* movie.

In *The Ultimates* #1, all but the last three pages take place in 1945, as we follow Captain America and his partner, Bucky. They lead a team to Iceland where the Nazis have finished building a missile that's aimed at the White House. Captain America jumps aboard the missile just as it's taking off, and, sacrificing himself, he sets off an explosive that destroys the missile and sends him plunging into the Arctic Ocean.

The Ultimates #1 is unusual, not only because it's the first issue of a team book that only shows one character, but also because it's essentially the origin story of the Ultimate version of Captain America, but we never see Steve Rogers injected with the serum that turned him into a super-soldier. Instead, we learn about him from the soldiers assigned to his platoon—who are skeptical about his abilities—and from a word balloon where he says, "I didn't go through six months on steroids and

The comic that kicks things off! *The Ultimates* #1 (March 2002), art by Bryan Hitch and Andrew Currie.

surgery so my fifteen-year-old brother could take a crash-course in German."

Millar likely assumes that even the most casual reader of comic books has a basic understanding of Captain America's origin and doesn't feel the need to spoon-feed them the info. Whatever the reason, it works. The issue is action-packed and already you have a good understanding of what motivates the Ultimate version of Captain America.

And the art is great. The double-page spread in #1, showing Captain America's team of soldiers charging towards a large Nazi scientific headquarters, is as cinematic as the D-Day scene from Steven Spielberg's *Saving Private Ryan*. Millar must have agreed, because the entire four-page sequence, showing the soldiers parachuting to the ground, the just-described double-page spread, and the beginning of the attack are all wordless. Millar lets the art tell the story. He knows how much Hitch and Currie bring to the story, telling *Wizard* in their September 2002 issue, "Everything I visualize when I'm writing is just multiplied by a thousand by the time it reaches the finished page."

This scene, and the entire series, is beautifully colored by Paul Mounts. His work helped establish the grounded, naturalistic approach that Hitch was bringing to his art. This photorealistic approach makes this super hero fantasy feel like it could be taking place in the real world.

Mounts uses natural muted colors and not the vibrant primary colors found in many super hero comics of this era. In this scene, which takes place at night, the lighting effects come from the explosions and bullet fire that are happening all around the soldiers. The night sky is dark and hazy, showing the pollution-like effects of the smoke from the many explosions.

Later in this issue, there's a splash page where Captain America is facing the reader and encouraging the soldiers to follow him, the right side of his body receiving light from an explosion that's happening behind him. The bullets hitting his shield are the brightest elements of the page.

As that scene moves into the Nazi headquarters, bullet fire

continues to be the primary light source. The muted colors again help with the photorealistic feel of the art. When the rocket ship that Captain America eventually destroys blasts off, the exhaust plume is the brightest thing we've seen in the issue. This contrast allows the reader to feel the power of the ship and the jeopardy Captain America faces. When Captain America successfully blows up the ship it's shown in a bright yellow blast, again emphasizing the power of the destruction.

This balance of spectacle and realism is extremely effective. Mounts' work perfectly matches the story Millar and Hitch

In a scene that rivals anything seen on a movie screen, U.S. soldiers attack a Nazi headquarters. *The Ultimates* #1 (March 2002), story by Mark Millar, art by Bryan Hitch and Andrew Currie.

are telling about real people—who, as we will see, are living in a version of our real world—who also just happen to be super heroes.

The last three pages of this issue fast forward to 2002, where Tony Stark has just reached the summit of Mt. Everest and announces he's going to start the next stage of his plan.

Before moving on to the second issue, it is worth noting that another unique feature of *The Ultimates* are the covers. Most super hero comic books feature a fight scene on the cover, a preview of the action inside. But as we've seen, there isn't a super hero fight in this issue or—as we're going to see—in the next couple of issues. So, the covers to *The Ultimates* feature the characters in heroic poses. This issue displays Captain America in color and in the front; the other characters on the team are behind him and only shown in silhouette.

Issue 2: "Big"

We start the second issue with a splash page set in New York City showing that one of the piers providing access to the Hudson River has been destroyed. We learn from General Nick Fury, as he's having a conversation over lunch with Bruce Banner, that this is Chelsea Piers, and it was destroyed by the Hulk.

In many Marvel comic books, there'd be a caption box telling

Captain America is revealed for the first time in the Ultimate universe. *The Ultimates* #1 (March 2002), story by Mark Millar, art by Bryan Hitch and Andrew Currie.

A flashback to the Hulk's origin that appeared in *Ultimate Marvel Team-Up*. *The Ultimates* #2 (April 2002), story by Mark Millar, art by Bryan Hitch and Andrew Currie.

the reader where this story happened. Something like "All you Ultimate fans remember this story from *Ultimate Marvel Team-Up* Nos. 2 & 3—Rascally Ralph." But instead of giving the info that way, *The Ultimates* creative team shows a panel of the Hulk battling Spider-Man, colored in a way to indicate it's a flashback. It's not necessary to have read those issues of *Ultimate Marvel Team-Up* to enjoy this story, but it's a nice Easter egg for anyone who has. It's also again setting an expectation for the reader that the creators aren't going to spoon-feed them the story. This is a comic book that warrants a little extra attention.

Bruce Banner is, of course, the Hulk, and Fury's lunch conversation also lets us know that Banner has been working on a super-soldier program for the last eight years—a program designed to create a new Captain America. It's an experiment as part of that program that causes Banner to turn into the Hulk.

We then move to "The Super-Soldier Research Facility" in Pittsburgh, where we meet Janet and Hank Pym. Hank made his first appearance as an Ultimate character in *Ultimate Spider-Man* #14, where he encountered the villain Doctor Octopus, who was briefly detained by the U.S. government.

In *The Ultimates* #2, Hank is using two and a half million ants to move boxes out of their office because they're going to be joining Banner in a facility off the coast of Manhattan. Hank will be Banner's boss, and he's ready to get started, saying, "The ideas for super-people are coming to me faster than I can type these days, Jan. This Giant Man formula is practically writing itself." While Janet and Hank are talking, she shrinks to the size of an action figure, and we can see she has wings.

The action then switches back to Manhattan, where Tony Stark meets with Nick Fury. It's quickly established that Stark is a genius who has a problem with alcohol. Stark and Fury discuss other possible additions to the team they're building—they'd like to add Thor, but he's been ghosting them. The Fantastic Four and X-Men are ruled out because they've both been getting negative press.

The origin story for the Ultimate version of Iron Man can be found in *Ultimate Marvel Team-Up* Nos. 4 and 5, written by Bendis with art by Michael Allred. Stark was a child prodigy

Tony Stark also made his first appearance in *Ultimate Marvel Team-Up* (July 2001), art by Mike Allred.

who "amassed a small personal fortune appearing on popular game shows." After dropping out of Harvard, he started Stark Industries. On a business trip to Guatemala, Stark and his cousin are kidnapped by terrorists who want him to build weapons for them. He does—building gloves with repulsor rays that he uses to defeat the terrorists. Stark escapes, but his cousin dies. After returning home, Stark avoids the public for two years. When he re-enters society, he has his Iron Man armor and immediately uses it to save the U.S. Vice President from an assassination attempt.

Stark never hid his identity, so by the time he joined the Ultimates, the public knew him and his Iron Man persona well. What the public doesn't know is that Stark is suffering from a degenerative brain tumor, and his Iron Man armor helps him manage his symptoms. Hitch described Iron Man this way to *Wizard* in their December 2001 issue: "This isn't a guy who carries around a super hero costume in a briefcase. This is a guy who needs a team of technicians to get him into his suit. He's launched from a silo, he's got a mission control team backing him—he's wearing a weapon."

In *The Ultimates* #2, we move to the Ultimates headquarters, called The Triskelion, where Banner and the Pyms are working. Some time must have passed because Hank is in the middle of running a Giant Man test on himself. Things look like they might be going wrong, but the experiment works, and Pym makes himself 59 feet, 11½ inches tall—exceeding 60 feet would have meant that his skeleton could no longer support his body mass.

The issue concludes with the revelation that Captain America's frozen body has been found in the Arctic Ocean. Unlike the first issue, which focused on the adventures of only one character, this one has all the members of what will become the Ultimates team, except for Thor. As Millar intended, it doesn't have any super-power fights; the closest we come to one is the single flashback panel showing the battle between the Hulk and Spider-Man.

Issue 3: 21st-Century Boy

Captain America, brought back to life after being frozen in ice for fifty-seven years, initially thinks Banner, Fury, and Stark are German imposters and breaks out of the hospital where he's been brought to recuperate. It takes Giant Man to subdue him before he can be convinced he's now in the future. Another shock is learning that his best friend, Bucky Barnes, married his fiancée, Gail Richards.

Millar brings a grounded and naturalistic approach to the dialogue throughout this series. We see an early example in an exchange between Nick Fury and Captain America,

The Triskelion! *The Ultimates* #3 (May 2002), story by Mark Millar, art by Bryan Hitch and Andrew Currie.

where Captain America is being told about how the world has changed.

> Fury: "It's you we're worried about right now, soldier. Are you absolutely sure this is the right time to put yourself through something like this, man?"
>
> Captain America: "Sir, I just found out my fiancée's married to my old best friend and they've got four kids and seven grandchildren. Let's be realistic here; there's never going to be a good time."
>
> Fury: "Fair point."

This approach to novelistic dialogue is further differentiated from other comic books on the market by the previously mentioned use of both lower- and upper-case letters.

The issue ends with an all-star opening night party for S.H.I.E.L.D.'s new team that, in addition to the superhumans, includes "five thousand technicians, [and] ten thousand support troops." Betty Ross, the public relations head for S.H.I.E.L.D. and Banner's estranged fiancée, tells Fury, "The difference between us and Hollywood, General, is that I'm going to make the Ultimates really famous." The party takes place on the Triskelion and Hitch uses a double-page spread to show us just how big it is.

The original Avengers also used the press to build interest in what they were doing. In 1965's *The Avengers* #16, much of the issue is devoted to press conferences—starting with one where Hawkeye is announced as a new team member and ending with one telling the public that Iron Man, Giant Man, and Wasp are taking a leave of absence and will be replaced by Quicksilver and Scarlet Witch.

Millar's script regularly refers to real-life people, firmly placing the Ultimates in the same world as the readers. The real world's President is shown at the S.H.I.E.L.D. party, and in a previous sequence, Fury makes a joke about an actor who would go on to later appear in the Marvel Cinematic Universe. Millar and Hitch weren't the first Marvel creators to use a real

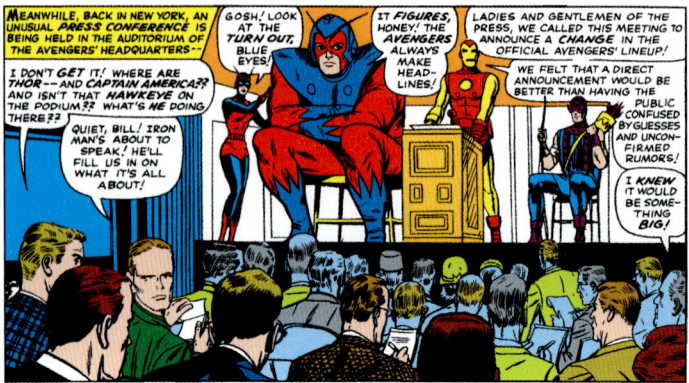

The first Avengers press conference. *The Avengers* #16 (May 1965), story by Stan Lee, art by Jack Kirby and Dick Ayers.

U.S. President in a story; President Franklin Roosevelt appeared in 1940's *Captain America Comics* #1, where he authorized the FBI to create the serum that turned Steve Rogers into the star-spangled super hero.

Issue 4: Thunder

The use of real people continues with the beginning of this issue, where we find Tony Stark in a spaceship with a popular actress of that era. And they're both being interviewed by a popular talk show host who had a show on CNN when this comic book was published. The pop culture references do make the series somewhat dated. I wonder if anyone in Generation Z would recognize either of these real-life people.

In any case, it's in this interview that we learn that it was Magento's attack on Washington D.C. that led the US government to fund the Ultimates program. During the interview, Stark is asked a question that readers might also be wondering about: "What if it's another ten years before someone like Magneto comes along? Supposing it never happens again?" In this unusual super hero team book, we're now into issue #4, and the only fight we've seen is the one that took place during World War II in issue #1 and the one Captain America started when he broke out of the hospital in issue #3.

Nick Fury wants more super heroes for the Ultimates, so he and Banner fly to Norway to recruit Thor. But the Ultimate version of Thor—who sounds like the modern-day Greta Thunberg—isn't interested and says, "Go back to your paymasters and tell them that the Son of Odin is not interested in working for a military industrial complex who engineers wars and murders innocents. Your talk might be of super-villains now, but it is only a matter of time before you are sent to kill for oil or free trade."

Banner walks in on the team while they're casting an *Ultimates* movie based on themselves and overhears them saying he could be played by Woody Allen or "that creepy little kid from *The Sixth Sense* or 'Stuart Little.'" He storms out of the room, and we cut to a scene in Times Square with Banner on the phone to Betty who's out to dinner with the actor Freddie

The Ultimates finally have a mission—take out the Hulk! *The Ultimates* #4 (April 2002), story by Mark Millar, art by Bryan Hitch and Andrew Currie.

Prinze, Jr. Banner tells her he's injected himself with a mixture of Captain America's blood and the Hulk serum. It's not long before Banner transforms into the Hulk and screams, "Hulk want Freddie Prince Junior!"

And finally, on the last page of this issue, we see the Ultimates team suited up for the first time, as Captain America tells the team they're going to hit the Hulk "until he drops."

Issue 5: Hulk Does Manhattan

As the team heads to Manhattan to take down the Hulk, we learn that Banner took the serum so the team would have "something newsworthy to fight." We also learn he left them the antidote they can use to stop him. Before the Ultimates can get there, Fury tells them Banner's poorly thought-out plan has already resulted in the death of dozens of people and mass destruction.

The slow build from the first issues is paid off with a scene that gives Hitch and Currie the chance to show their super hero chops with three splash pages and a double-page spread that shows the deranged Hulk screaming "Bettyyyy!!" This pivot from the character-driven scenes we've seen in the earlier issues to this massive fight scene pushes super hero storytelling into blockbuster movie territory. The Hulk's destructive rampage

The Hulk only has one thing on his mind! *The Ultimates* #5 (July 2002), story by Mark Millar, art by Bryan Hitch and Andrew Currie.

through Manhattan is right out of a Hollywood disaster movie. It's this combination of deep character work—where we've seen Banner unleashing the Hulk out of jealousy and insecurity—and cinematic art that makes this series stand out.

Discussing his work on the series, Hitch said in the September 2002 of *Wizard*, "I enjoy doing the big fight scenes, but the real challenge is to bring to life our characters. I can be as excited about drawing the façade of St. Patrick's Cathedral as I can be about the Hulk laying into Thor."

Speaking of Thor, he shows up after the entire Ultimates

team has been individually defeated by the Hulk, and the President agrees to double the U.S.'s international aid budget. Thor and his hammer, Mjolnir, also fail to stop the Hulk. It's up to the Wasp to save the day. After an unfortunate scene where she tried to distract the raging beast by showing him her bare breasts, she shrinks to a size that allows her to enter the Hulk's body to give him "a little wasp sting to the portion of his brain that makes him big, bad and angry."

The comic ends with a scene where Captain America and the Wasp find Bruce Banner in the middle of some of the wreckage his alter ego caused. Millar's dialogue continues to flesh out the characters he's writing about—in this case, Captain America's uncompromising approach to justice and the insecurity of Bruce Banner.

Banner begs for mercy, saying, "I was only trying to help. This was all part of the plan, you see. I was only trying to come up with a menace you could all get together and fight …" Captain America responds, "I'm just here to make sure those cuts and bruises of yours get the proper attention, pal. C'mere, let me get a closer look at that big gash on your cheek …" There is no gash—until Captain America kicks him in the face.

Millar is again letting readers know this is the Ultimate version of *The Avengers*.

Issue 6: Giant Man vs. the Wasp

The Triskelion has converted its lobby into an emergency hospital for people injured in the Hulk's attack on Manhattan. After walking through the injured and dying people, General Fury and Betty Ross head to the room holding Banner. Along the way, Fury asks Ross how they're going to stop the media from reporting the fact that it was a member of their own team that caused the disaster. She tells him, "Oh, come on now, Nick. That's easy—just hush up the Bruce Banner connection and all your little super people here go down in history as the heroes who saved Manhattan, of course."

To that effect, Captain America and Iron Man do live TV interviews in the middle of the carnage. A visibly battered Captain America says he has broken ribs, a broken nose, and a dislocated arm but that he'll be fine in a day or two. When Iron Man is asked if he was scared, he tells the reporter, "To tell you the truth, I was shaking like a leaf, my dear. If it wasn't for the fact I'd downed a few glasses of the old Dutch courage at a wine-tasting this evening, I honestly think I might have called in sick." The crowd behind him cheers and throws their arms in the air in support.

This issue came out almost a year after the 9/11 terrorist attacks that brought down the Twin Towers in the same city the Hulk had just rampaged through. While those attacks are never directly mentioned—it's Magneto's attack on Washington D.C. that led to the formation of the Ultimates—they would be top of mind for the readers who bought this off the racks in August 2002. For readers in 2002, the Ultimates provides a powerful fantasy—a world where super-soldiers will save the people of the United States from the unexpected.

While Thor, Captain America, and Iron Man meet for a dinner at Tony Stark's place on Park Avenue, Hank and Janet Pym—who were also expected to attend the dinner—are about to have the most disturbing scene in the series.

In *The Avengers* #213 (November 1981), Hank Pym, who was facing a court martial by his Avengers teammates because of his erratic behavior, strikes his wife in the face. This was a controversial storyline when it appeared, and rather than shy away from it in this reimagined version of the Giant Man character, Millar took it even further. *The Ultimates* version of Hank Pym—embarrassed by how soundly he was beaten by the Hulk and jealous of a picture showing the Wasp kissing Captain America—attacks Janet. She fights back and, to get away, shrinks and flies away. Hank sprays her with bug spray and uses his ants to attack her, saying, "You shouldn't have made me look small, Jan."

In the conversation that leads up to the attack, we also learn that Janet Pym is a mutant. Her powers aren't the result of something Hank invented—she was born with them. Before the

Hank Pym's worst moment. *The Ultimates* #6 (August 2002), story by Mark Millar, art by Bryan Hitch and Andrew Currie.

issue, and this story arc, ends, we are also reminded that Tony Stark has a brain tumor that gives him "between six months and five years" to live and that Thor is a "God made man … the living incarnation of a Norse thunder deity sent here by my father in Valhalla to purify the Earth again."

The Reaction

To differentiate it from other Marvel comic books of the era, every issue of *The Ultimates* was printed with a cardstock cover and glossy paper. The upgraded physical product paired with exceptional storytelling worked. *The Ultimates* #1 was the bestselling comic book of 2002 and the subsequent five issues were all easily in the top 50 comics of the year (#2 at #22, #3 at #26, #4 at #35, #5 at #33, and #6 at #42). *The Ultimates* Volume 1, which collects issues one to six, was the twenty-fifth bestselling book of 2002, getting beaten by all three volumes of *Ultimate Spider-Man*, which had Volume 1 at #5, Volume 2 at #18, and Volume 3 at #20. In 2003, *The Ultimates* Volume 1 moved up to the #12 spot.

In their November 2002 issue, *Wizard* called *The Ultimates* the "Book of the Month" and said, "With a combustible combination of character-driven plots that'll keep your stomach in knots eventually giving way to cinematic super hero action that hammers you over the head, *The Ultimates* is quickly gaining stature as the benchmark for super hero books."

In their January 2003 issue, *Wizard* would go on to pick *The Ultimates* as the "Best Comic" of 2002, remarking, "With heaping helpings of realism, controversy and mind-blowing art, *The Ultimates* clearly stands as not only the best book of the year, but the most powerful take on Marvel's Ultimate concept yet."

Bryan Hitch and Andrew Currie were nominated as "Best Penciller/Inker or Penciller/Inker or Penciller/Inker Team" in the 2003 Eisner Awards.

In the 10th Annual Wizard Fan Awards, Mark Millar was nominated as "Favorite Writer" but lost to his fellow Ultimate writer Brian Michael Bendis. Hitch was also nominated as "Favorite Penciller" and the series was nominated as "Favorite Ongoing Series." It lost, again to *Ultimate Spider-Man*. Chris Eliopoulos won the "Favorite Letterer" award, and a scene where Captain America took out the Hulk in *The Ultimates* No. 5 won for "Comics Greatest Moment."

Hitch was again nominated as "Favorite Penciller" at the 11th Annual Wizard Fan Awards. Chris Eliopoulos won "Favorite Letterer" again and Ralph Macchio won as "Favorite Editor" for his work on the Ultimate titles. Millar was nominated in the 12th Annual Wizard Fan Awards for "Best Writer," while Chris Eliopoulos and Ralph Macchio won again that year.

The scene that was named "Comics Greatest Moment" of 2002. *The Ultimates* #5 (July 2002), story by Mark Millar, art by Bryan Hitch and Andrew Currie.

Saint Patrick's Cathedral, New York City. *The Ultimates* #7 (September 2002), story by Mark Millar, art by Bryan Hitch and Andrew Currie.

6

The Ultimates—Homeland Security!

Issue 7

This issue and issue 9 don't have titles. One thing that continued was an intro page, something that started with the second issue. The intro page has a headshot of all the team members at the top and a short recap of the story. It also features an establishing shot by Hitch and Currie. This issue's image is a bird's-eye view of Saint Patrick's Cathedral in New York City. The image on the first page of the story is also of Saint Patrick's Cathedral, this time from a view slightly above ground level and drawn in a beautiful photo-realistic style.

When describing his artistic approach in his book *Bryan Hitch's Ultimate Comics Studio*, Hitch emphasized that establishing shots like the one just described were important to him,

Not all comic artists are keen to show the reality of the environment in which the story is set, but to me it is an important part of the storytelling process. It makes the reader feel involved and helps to achieve verisimilitude. If a story is set in New York then I want the reader to experience the awe of walking around Manhattan. I want big shots of the city, which I research using a variety of books and bespoke photographic reference.

The story heads inside the church where Captain America is giving a eulogy for the people killed by the Hulk. As he speaks, we also see Janet Pym being taken by ambulance to a hospital. Meanwhile, Bruce Banner is in a cell where he learns S.H.I.E.L.D. isn't telling the public he's the Hulk because "we couldn't exactly have the brains behind America's twenty-first century defense initiative be the target of their first big public operation." The Ultimates' first fight is a big PR win for the group.

That doesn't last, as the team and the media learn that Janet's in the hospital and that Hank's the one responsible for putting her there. We learn from Betty that this isn't the first time it's happened. She knew them in college, and he hit her back then. It isn't long before the media starts broadcasting the story.

The issue ends with the introduction of two other S.H.I.E.L.D. operatives, Black Widow and Hawkeye, who work for the Black Ops team. Both characters are only seen in one

Black Widow enters the story. *The Ultimates* #7 (April 2005), art by Bryan Hitch and Andrew Currie.

panel in the issue, but the Black Widow is featured on the cover. Like the other covers in the series, this one focuses on a close-up of the Black Widow. She's hanging upside down with her red hair flowing towards the ground. She holds a pistol and has a Black Widow emblem on her chest. She doesn't get any action scenes in this issue, but we can tell from the cover that this is likely going to change.

One contemporary reviewer of issue 7 remarked that "Some people may be disappointed that there are no characters in bright colors hitting one another. No doubt there will be plenty of that in future issues. But in this case, writer Mark Millar[,] with the talents of Bryan Hitch (pencils) and Andrew Currie (inks), tells a tale as strong and potentially as real as anything else on the stands today."[10]

Issue 8: The Experts

This issue's focus is on Black Widow and Hawkeye, both characters that go back to the earliest days of Marvel's history.

Like Hulk and Iron Man, the Ultimate version of Black Widow made her first appearance in the Ultimate universe in an issue of *Ultimate Marvel Team-Up*, which came out six months before *The Ultimates* #8. In that story, written by Bendis with art by *Strangers in Paradise* creator Terry

Moore and inker Walden Wong, we learn her real name is Natasha Romanov and that she's a descendant of Russia's royal family. She was trained to be a spy by the KGB, and her wrist cartridges and belt have "tear-gas pellets, a radio transmitter and spring-loaded cables, as well as a small device capable of emitting a high-frequency electrostatic charge." She also has "microscopic suction cups built into her uniform [that] enable the Widow to walk on walls and ceilings." The story ends with General Fury taking her away in a S.H.I.E.L.D. helicopter and a caption that reads, "See more of Black Widow in the pages of *The Ultimates*."

This is all similar to the character who appears in the regular Marvel universe. That version—created by writers Stan Lee and Don Rico, and artist Don Heck—got her start way back in 1964 in *Tales of Suspense* #52, where she was sent by the Russians to distract Iron Man with her beauty so her counterparts could steal his technology.

In her early appearances, she's dressed as a glamorous socialite, and it was in her third appearance in *Tales of Suspense* #57 that she would meet Hawkeye. He was making his first appearance in the Marvel Universe, and the pair teamed up to take on Iron Man. In her fifth appearance, in *Tales of Suspense* #64, she donned a costume for the first time. Hawkeye became a good guy and joined The Avengers, and in *The Avengers* #30, Black Widow stopped that issue's bad guys from killing him.

She claimed she'd broken through the brainwashing she'd been subjected to by the "Reds."

From that point forward she was a super hero, eventually switching to a costume similar to the one she wears in *The Ultimates*. Her stories were told in *Amazing Adventures*—also featuring The Inhumans—which made Black Widow the first stand-alone female super hero series in the modern era of Marvel Comics. And just like her Ultimate version, she worked for Nick Fury and S.H.I.E.L.D. and even joined The Avengers, where she led the team for three years.

The Ultimate versions of Black Widow and Hawkeye start issue 8 by entering an office building in downtown New York City with a strike team of S.H.I.E.L.D. soldiers. They wantonly kill everyone in the building, and Black Widow shows off her undefined "four million dollar enhancements" by jumping from an upper window of one building, catching a gun dropped to her by a helicopter, and landing on the demolished floor of another building.

Millar again lets the art tell most of the story in this action sequence and, as usual, Hitch doesn't disappoint. In the middle of the action there's a splash page of a New York City street with massive skyscrapers. The buildings are drawn in such detail, we feel like we can almost see into them. One of those buildings is shown with an explosion happening over four or five of its upper floors. The next page is a three-panel one where

Black Widow in her groundbreaking series, *Amazing Adventures*. *Amazing Adventures* #1 (August 1970), art by Jack Kirby and John Romita.

we see Black Widow reacting to the explosion followed by the wreckage from the blast hitting the busy New York street below.

It's an action-packed twelve-page sequence, but we don't learn much about why S.H.I.E.L.D. initiated this attack other than hearing that there are "sleeper-agents" in the building.

After the fight, Fury introduces Black Widow and Hawkeye to Thor and Iron Man and reveals that Quicksilver and Scarlet Witch—who first met Nick Fury in *Ultimate X-Men*—are also joining the Ultimates as part of a "Shadow Team." Like the original Marvel versions of those characters—who joined *The Avengers* in #16—they're siblings who previously worked for Magneto's Brotherhood of Mutants and are also that supervillain's children. They're also the characters featured on this issue's cover.

In *The Ultimates*, they've agreed to work for S.H.I.E.L.D. in "exchange for the release of political prisoners." The mutant siblings don't do much in this story arc, or at least not anything we can see. The running joke (pun intended) is that Quicksilver is moving so fast his teammates never see how he's helping. It's another example of the humor Millar brings to this work—offsetting potentially world-ending conflicts with humorous banter between the characters and his willingness to let some of the action happen off of the page.

After Black Widow questions whether or not Quicksilver actually did anything on the mission, Quicksilver responds,

Black Widow showing off her "four million dollar enhancements." *The Ultimates* #8 (November 2002), story by Mark Millar, art by Bryan Hitch and Paul Neary.

"Actually, if you slow down the building's security tapes, I think you'll find that I saved your lives on three separate occasions, you ungrateful sow." Black Widow, with a smirk on her face, responds simply with "liar."

Fury tells the team that Earth has eleven different alien species on it. The ones they're concerned about are the Chitauri, who have been on Earth a long time. The natural form of a Chitauri has a reptilian appearance, and they have a height of over eight feet, but they can transform themselves to look like humans. They infiltrated Nazi Germany, and when the Allied forces won World War II, it was assumed all of the aliens had been destroyed.

Captain America obviously fought the Chitauri during the war, but he's not at the meeting where they're being discussed. He's tracked down Hank Pym and prepares to confront him about what he did to Janet.

Paul Neary

Paul Neary—another UK citizen—replaced Andrew Currie as inker on issue #9. Neary got his start with the black-and-white horror anthology comic magazines *Eerie* and *Creepy* in the early 1970s. He made the switch to Marvel UK in 1979, where he provided the covers for the British titles that reprinted US Marvel comics. Among the titles he worked on were *Hulk*

Comic and *Captain America*. When he started working for Marvel Comics, Neary had a long run as *Captain America*'s penciller, working on the title from 1984 to 1987. All of this gave him an early start on the characters he would be tackling in *The Ultimates*.

In the early 1990s, Neary became the editor-in-chief of Marvel UK before spending most of the rest of his career as an inker.

Issue 9

The first half of this issue is devoted to a fight between Captain America and Hank Pym. Hitch's storytelling is extraordinary, particularly in a four-page sequence that sees Captain America soundly beating Pym even when he's changed size to become Giant Man. Captain America proves it can be brains and not just brawn that can win a fight. He's also not afraid of a quality one-liner as he ends the fight by asking Giant Man, "How big do you feel now?"

After defeating her husband, Captain America goes to visit Janet in the hospital. He doesn't get the reception he expected, as Janet tells him, "Any problems Hank and I are having right now aren't going to be helped by you making a fool of yourself

Even at his giant size, Hank Pym can't beat Captain America. *The Ultimates* #9 (April 2003), story by Mark Millar, art by Bryan Hitch and Paul Neary.

and acting like some idiot knight in shining armor. This isn't 1945, Steve. This isn't how you fix things anymore."

Bruce Banner is held in a cell on The Triskelion and when Betty tells him that Captain America broke Hank Pym's jaw, he says, "That's the greatest thing I've ever heard." Millar also uses this scene to poke fun at conspiracy theories of that era, when he has Betty tell Banner, "I know it's nuts, but there's a rumor flying around that this is part of some big drive to get kids microchipped and more compliant with whatever the alien agenda is."

The rest of issue #9 is devoted to the Chitauris and their alien agenda. We learn they're in Micronesia with "a radar-invisible, twenty-mile-wide facility with thousands of grunts and a wide selection of doomsday weapons."

Millar and Hitch continue to show us the scenes that most super hero comics ignore. In this case, it's a sequence with Black Widow and Iron Man discussing their fears about the upcoming mission. They're on the "Iron-Tech launch pad" and Hitch's detailed art emphasizes the enormous size of the facility and the complexity of what they're planning to do.

When Tony tells Natasha he's nervous about the upcoming missions she says, "You see Hawkeye over there? Did you know that he telephones his girlfriend and says goodbye to his children before every single mission just in case it's his last?" Tony responds, "A tad morbid, don't you think?"

And Natasha says, "No, because one day it will be his last, comrade."

This quiet scene is Millar at his best. It allows the readers to think of the characters as more than just the suits and powers they bring to fights. They're real people who are willing to put their lives in jeopardy to save others. They're heroes.

The scene also foreshadows for the readers that not all of the characters may survive the upcoming fight. As Captain America rejoins the rest of the team, they head to Micronesia to kill the aliens. They're finally going into a battle that isn't against one of their teammates.

Issue 10: Devil in Disguise

Things get off to a bang this time around as we flash back to 1944. Captain America is in Poland on top of a train that's carrying parts for a secret Nazi super weapon. Standing on the train with him is a Nazi officer who taunts Captain America because he thinks he's failed in his mission. He hasn't. Captain America jumps off the train just as the bombs he planted explode. Captain America doesn't hear him, but the Nazi curses in an alien tongue before—presumably—dying.

Hitch's storytelling in this sequence is again as good as super hero comic books get. It starts with an establishing splash page

Hitch's storytelling is as good as it gets. *The Ultimates* #10 (July 2003), story by Mark Millar, art by Bryan Hitch and Paul Neary.

where we see the train and the characters. The rest of the panels in the sequence are multi-panel ones, all designed to clearly show the placement of the characters and the ticking bomb. All of this is done in the photorealistic style Hitch always uses.

In his book *Bryan Hitch's Ultimate Comics Studio* and the section on drawing comic books—titled "Rhythm of storytelling"—Hitch describes his approach this way:

> I use the word "rhythm" in a musical sense. Rhythm and beats are used in music to speed things up and slow them down—music has loud bits and quiet bits. Comic books have that as well, and the number of panels you use for a story, the size you use them at and the order they go in all help to create the story's rhythm and pace. The big image is the crescendo, and the smaller preceding images are all building up to the big moment, with subsequent ones providing the quieter rhythms.

Millar is also in rhythm with Hitch's use of panel size and placement. Many pages have no text at all, allowing Hitch to tell the story on his own. The sequence described above starts with a splash page that only has one word balloon. It's followed by a multi-panel page that carries most of the dialogue in which the bad guy overshares about his plan. It ends with Captain America telling him they're on to him and he's going to blow up the train. The next page has ten panels, with only the first and

Millar and Hitch are in "rhythm" with their storytelling. *The Ultimates* #10 (July 2003), story by Mark Millar, art by Bryan Hitch and Paul Neary.

last having any text. The other panels build tension by showing us the bombs Captain America planted. The sequence ends with a page that has four horizontal panels where the villain realizes he's in trouble and ends with the train exploding.

The story then advances to 1945 as Captain America meets with U.S. military leaders who tell him the Nazi officer from the train is still alive. It's here we learn that the U.S. and Captain America know about the aliens. He learns "that these spacemen have kick-started the Nazi nuclear program again and the North Atlantic seems to be at the heart of it." Captain America also learns the aliens are hard to kill when General Eisenhower

S.H.I.E.L.D. has arrived. *The Ultimates* #10 (July 2003), story by Mark Millar, art by Bryan Hitch and Paul Neary.

tells him, "Unfortunately, you aren't the only one out there with nine lives."

Flashing forward to the present day, we see the massive airships Fury is bringing to Micronesia for the battle with the Chitauris in a double-page spread that's as good as anything you've seen on a movie screen. Hitch and Neary show us dozens of planes and ships—some as small as fighter jets and some as large as floating battleships. As we've seen before, the detail is extraordinary. It's so real, it feels photorealistic but, of course, most of the ships don't exist in the real world, so no photo could be taken of them.

Meanwhile, Janet's still in the hospital on The Triskelion when she discovers the Chitauris have replaced all the humans. She barely escapes by shrinking to her wasp size and flying into an air vent.

Fury and the Ultimates arrive in Micronesia to learn there are no aliens there. It was a trap. Now that the Ultimates and 20,000 soldiers are on the island, the Chitauris set off an atomic bomb, obliterating the island and all the massive aircraft we saw earlier.

In showing the destruction from the bomb, Hitch stages the storytelling in a way that starts small with a group of soldiers on the ground. We see them looking at a bomb counter that's just ticked down to zero. One of them says, "Oh, my god." In the next two panels we see the results of the explosion. In the

Things aren't looking good for our heroes! *The Ultimates* #10 (July 2003), story by Mark Millar, art by Bryan Hitch and Paul Neary.

first, the soldiers have been reduced to skeletons. In the second, they've been completely obliterated, removed from the face of the Earth. Both of those panels are colored in a phosphorescent green that makes us think of nuclear waste. The next panel establishes a view of the horizon where we can see the globe-like impact of the nuclear blast.

The next page has four horizontal panels where we see the impact of the blast on the ships and ends with a bird's-eye view of the nuclear blast. The explosion is shown as a globe with expanding concentric circles—an image familiar to anyone who has seen a nuclear blast in a movie or documentary. Other than the first panel, there's no text. Millar again lets Hitch tell the story, and he does it well.

Issue 11: The Art of War

This issue opens with a splash page that shows the wrecked airships in Micronesia before quickly switching back to The Triskelion, which is now partly under Chitauri control. The Nazi officer Captain America fought on the train back in 1944 is in charge of the alien troops. Going by the name Kleiser, the same one he used when he was a Nazi, the Chitauri leader tracks down Janet Pym. When she shrinks down to her wasp size, he grabs her by her wings and puts her in a test tube.

In classic bad guy behavior, Kleiser tells Janet their plans. The Chitauri aren't just invading Earth, they're putting the entire galaxy back into order. And they've been doing it "since the dawn of time." For humans, this means removing their free will by putting mood suppressants in the drinking water.

They also plan a microchipping program in "the next stage of the mobile phone revolution." Bear in mind that this was published in 2003—four years before the first iPhone—when Kleiser says, "By the end of the decade, I doubt there will be a person alive who'll be capable of forming a coherent independent thought." I'll let you decide if this story was prescient or not.

Kleiser and Janet then fly to Arizona where the aliens have a series of military hangars in the desert, which they've chosen to decorate with Nazi flags. Kleiser tells her, "They're really more of a symbolic thing anyway. I like to think of it as marking our territory again after all those years of hiding in the jungles." Janet asks why he's kept the German name and learns that the aliens become the people they eat and that he's planning to have her as his next meal.

While all this villain-splaining is going on, hundreds of alien ships suddenly appear in the sky. Kleiser learns that his plans for Earth are finished. The Chitauri battles throughout the universe are going poorly, so they're going to cut their losses and just destroy the third planet from the sun.

Those ships didn't last long. *The Ultimates* #11 (September 2003), story by Mark Millar, art by Bryan Hitch and Paul Neary.

In another surprise, Kleiser discovers that the Ultimates weren't destroyed in the Micronesia explosion. Iron Man had a force field that saved them, and they've just arrived on the scene to battle the aliens.

This issue really allows Hitch and Neary to shine. Using the "rhythm of storytelling" described above, the issue starts with a splash page of the downed ships in Micronesia before switching to five multi-panel pages that allow Millar to tell the reader what the bad guys are doing. When the alien ships are shown arriving on Earth, we begin with a multi-panel page where we see pilots, regular citizens on the ground, and soldiers all looking at something we can't quite see. When the page is turned it's a double-page spread where we see what they've been looking at—dozens of massive alien ships in the sky.

As the Ultimates prepare to go into battle, another double-page spread shows our heroes armed and ready for action. Captain America is in the front and says, "Tony? Thor? Lead the charge." The next two pages are multi-panel ones where the fight commences, and the issue ends with a splash page of Captain America about to enter a plane. He's been using a headset to tell the military personnel about the mission and ends by saying, "Your country needs you." He's speaking to the people fighting with him but because he's looking directly at the reader, he's also speaking to us.

In a sign of the success of the series, this issue has a full-page ad for an action figure based on the Ultimate version of the Hulk, produced by Diamond Select Toys. Other Ultimates figures in the line included Captain America, Iron Man, and Thor. Diamond Select Toys would also go on to create statues and busts of those same characters.

Issue 12: Persons of Mass Destruction

This issue lets Hitch and Neary shine with nearly non-stop action throughout. Hitch again does a spectacular job, starting with a double-page spread of Thor destroying one of the alien ships with his hammer. That's followed by a multi-page sequence of Captain America fighting Kleiser. Hitch's photo-realism, combined with individual panels that capture each punch and kick, brings the reader right into the action.

As the ship at the center of the action begins to explode, Hitch and Neary show the destruction in detail. Unfortunately, that massive ship is set to crash into downtown Phoenix until Iron Man, using all of his power, diverts it away from the city.

Captain America and Kleiser continue their fight, and just as it looks like America's avenger is about to be killed, he rallies and takes out the alien leader. The fight ends with what is probably the best-known image from the series—a splash page of Captain America, pointing to the A on his forehead as he says, "You think this letter on my head stands for France?"

To put this in context, around the time the comic book was published, some people in the U.S. were mad at France because they opposed the U.S. invasion of Iraq. Some members of Congress went so far as saying that French Fries should be renamed Freedom Fries.

A few years later, in a *Captain America* series written by Ed Brubaker that was based in the regular Marvel Universe, Captain America has a multi-page sequence where he tells someone how brave the French were during World War II. Some fans believe this was Brubaker's response to the story in *The Ultimates*.

Getting back to the story, even though Captain America has won his fight, the alien bombs haven't been stopped. Fury desperately authorizes his soldiers to "traumatize Banner." We learn that Banner is in a helicopter with a platoon of soldiers who start beating the crap out of him. It doesn't work; Banner doesn't change into the Hulk, so they go with "plan B" and throw him out the side of the helicopter. The issue ends as Banner starts to plummet to the ground screaming, "No!"

That scene is depicted in a splash page that Hitch frames in a way so that Banner and the helicopter he has just been tossed out of are at the top of the page. The bottom half of the page has nothing other than a few small shards of broken glass. This

Captain America may still be holding a grudge about France surrendering to Germany during World War II. *The Ultimates* #12 (November 2003), story by Mark Millar, art by Bryan Hitch and Paul Neary.

is effective storytelling because it allows the reader to imagine that Banner's fall looks like it will be endless. It's another example of the writer and artist working in sync. Millar doesn't fill the page with unnecessary captions and dialogue; he allows Hitch to give all the necessary storytelling information to the reader.

Issue 13: How I Learned to Love the Hulk

This is the only issue of *The Ultimates* to have a content rating on it. In 2003, Marvel implemented a new system that had four levels: All Ages (8+ years old), Marvel PSR (Parental Supervision Recommended, 12+ years old), Marvel PSR+ (15+ years old), and Parental Advisory/Explicit Content (18+ years old). *The Ultimates* #13 fell into the Marvel PSR+ category.

It's also the first issue since issue #1 to feature the entire team on the cover. Unlike that cover, which only showed Captain America in detail, this one shows all of the characters. Captain America is again the featured character, but Giant Man, Iron Man, the Wasp, and even Hawkeye and Black Widow are all easily recognizable. However, it's still not the typical fight scene we'd expect on a super hero comic book. On this cover, it appears the heroes are standing victorious in the ruins of a building.

In an extra-long story that picks up straight from the end of the previous issue, Banner crashes into a building, with the destruction again shown in explicit detail by Hitch and Neary. An enormous Hulk then explodes out of the building in a double-page spread that can't contain the character, with both of his arms going past the printed pages.

In typical villain fashion, Captain America and Nick Fury discover Kleiser is still alive. Rather than fight him again, Captain America tells Hulk the alien has been bragging about being with Betty. An enraged Hulk picks up Kleiser by the foot and smashes him over and over into the ground. Hulk screams, "Naked guy went and made Hulk angry!!" After beating him some more, Hulk eventually tears Kleiser's head off and eats him.

While all that's going on, Wasp and Black Widow are trying to deactivate the bomb, and Thor is in the sky taking out alien spaceships. Now that Kleiser is truly dead, Captain America—using a slur that hasn't stood the test of time—tricks Hulk into helping Thor with the spaceships.

Thor and Iron Man join Wasp and Black Widow as they try to figure out what to do with the alien bomb they can't deactivate. Iron Man comes up with the idea of having Thor transport it to "some mystical realm." Black Widow skeptically asks, "Are you serious? You're going to take the bomb and dump it in Narnia?"—but it works. (Thor actually takes it to

You really don't want to make the Hulk angry. *The Ultimates* #13 (September 2003), story by Mark Millar, art by Bryan Hitch and Paul Neary.

"the wastes of Nastrond.") Yeah, it's a classic example of *deus ex machina*, but there's a reason that plot device has been used for thousands of years—it's effective.

After the fight ends, we have a panel featuring the entire Ultimates team—Thor, Iron Man, Captain America, Nick Fury, Scarlet Witch, Black Widow, and Hawkeye. As we saw on the cover, they're all facing the reader but in this shot its Black Widow in the center. She says, "I think this means we're officially super heroes now."

The story ends with the team being invited to a party at the White House to celebrate their victory. Janet, who sensibly broke up with Hank via phone, dances with Captain America. She tells him she's sorry she got mad at him earlier. The last page shows Nick Fury exiting the Oval Office and saying, "Ain't every day we save the world," as fireworks explode over the White House.

And with that, *The Ultimates* comes to an end. Looking back at this series, popular Marvel writer Jonathan Hickman said, "I think The Ultimates Volume 1 is about as perfect as big event mainstream comics can be done."[11]

Ultimate Avengers (2006)

In the mid-2000s, Marvel did a deal with Lions Gate Entertainment to produce direct-to-DVD animated movies. A total of eight movies were released, with the first one being *Ultimate Avengers*. Loosely based on *The Ultimates*, Mark Millar and Bryan Hitch get an on-screen credit at the beginning of the movie.

The movie is rated PG-13, and while only the last issue of *The Ultimates* had a rating of PSR+ (15+ year olds), the comics are written and drawn with an older audience in mind. Almost none of Millar's dialogue and character development made it into the movie.

The main fight is still against the aliens, but Kleiser is only seen in the initial scene that takes place during World War II. So there's no longer a personal battle with Captain America, and Captain America never says his line about the A on his head. Hank doesn't attack Janet. Stark's identity is secret through most of the story. The Black Widow is in the story from the beginning, while Hawkeye, Quicksilver, and Scarlet Witch aren't in it at all.

There was a sequel, *Ultimates Avengers 2: Rise of the Panther*, that takes a couple of plot points from *The Ultimates*, but it's mostly a new story. In the movie, Kleiser and the Chitauri return to further threaten the Earth. After initially fighting each other, the Ultimates and Black Panther team up to defeat them.

There's also an episode of the animated series *Avengers Assemble*, titled "The Ultimates," in which Ultron creates robot versions of the Avengers characters. The heroes have to fight their doppelgangers before they can save the day. Some of the costumes appear to be loosely based on Hitch's designs but the story has nothing to do with *The Ultimates*.

There are also two prose novels that take place between *The Ultimates* and *The Ultimates 2*—*The Ultimates: Tomorrow Men*, written by Michael Jan Friedman, and *The Ultimates: Against All Enemies*, written by Alex Irvine. Iron Man travels through time in *Tomorrow Men*, and the Chitauri return again in *Against All Enemies*. Both novels are also available as audiobooks that feature a full cast, music, and sound effects.

7
Interlude: Ultimate Galactus

In a story that was originally planned to be written by Millar and that takes place between *The Ultimates* and *The Ultimates 2*, writer Warren Ellis—another British citizen—introduces the Ultimate Galactus in a trilogy of mini-series.

Galactus, the cosmic devourer of worlds, made his first appearance in *Fantastic Four* Nos. 48–50 (1966), a legendary three-issue storyline known as "*The Galactus Trilogy*." Written by Stan Lee and illustrated by Jack Kirby, this famous story introduced Galactus as an omnipotent cosmic entity who arrives on Earth to consume its life energy. Accompanied by his herald, the Silver Surfer, Galactus is a global threat more powerful than anything the Fantastic Four have ever faced. As the team scrambles to stop him, the Silver Surfer, inspired by the nobility of humanity, turns against his master. To win

Captain America and Black Widow team up with some of the other Ultimate characters. *Ultimate Nightmare* #1 (October 2004), art by Trevor Hairsine.

the battle, the Fantastic Four's leader, Reed Richards, uses the Ultimate Nullifier, a weapon capable of erasing even Galactus.

"The Galactus Trilogy" expanded the scale of Marvel's universe and showed Lee and Kirby working at the top of their form.

The Ultimate version of "The Galactus Trilogy" starts with *Ultimate Nightmare*, where Ellis pairs up with artists Trevor Hairsine, Nelson DeCastro, and Simon Coleby to tell a horror story where Fury, Captain America, and Black Widow track down an alien presence that's causing havoc all over the world. Along the way, the Ultimate version of Falcon is introduced, and the Ultimates characters get in a fight with some of the Ultimate X-Men.

In *Ultimate Secret*, Ellis and artists Steve McNiven, Tom Raney, Mark Morales, and Scott Hanna tell a story that features Fury, Iron Man, Thor, Black Widow, and Hawkeye. They team up with the Fantastic Four and a Kree alien—who goes by the name Mahr Vehl—as they race to get the secrets they need to defeat Gah Lak Tus from a Kree spaceship. This series spends time developing the friendship and partnership between Hawkeye and Black Widow which—as we'll see—makes one of the plots in *The Ultimates 2* even more heartbreaking.

In *Ultimate Extinction*, the concluding series, Ellis is joined by artist Brandon Peterson. It starts with Reed Richards updating Fury and others—including Mahr Vehl, who now goes

The Falcon joins the story. *Ultimate Nightmare* #2 (November 2004), story by Warren Ellis, art by Trevor Hairsine, Nelson DeCastro, and Simon Coleby.

by the title Captain Marvel—on the Gah Lak Tus threat. The attack will start with a psychic blast that will drive the entire world mad. Next will come a flesh-eating virus that will kill everyone. And then it'll wrap up with Gah Lak Tus essentially breaking the planet open to steal its energy before moving on to its next target.

We also meet the Ultimate version of Silver Surfer, who is representative of a group of silver men that can manifest wings that make them look somewhat like very shiny angels. They've inspired death cults all over the world. The goal of Gah Lak Tus is to kill as many of the inhabitants of a planet as possible before it arrives to suck out all the energy.

Gah Lak Tus is eventually defeated by a two-pronged attack: Professor X and Jean Grey of the X-Men hit it with a massive psychic blast while Reed Richards hits it with a giant laser beam. Gah Lak Tus hates interacting with anything that lives, so it decides to find a planet that'll cause him less trouble.

While it's not necessary to read this story to enjoy *The Ultimates 2*, it's a well written crossover with nice art. Ellis brings a cerebral approach to the story, incorporating real world events like the Tunguska event—an asteroid explosion that occurred over Russia in 1908—and the Fermi Paradox—which describes the contradiction between the high probability of alien civilizations existing in our universe and the fact that we haven't encountered them.

In addition to his more serious storytelling, Ellis also doesn't include as much humor or as many pop culture references as Millar. I like both approaches.

The Ultimates are back in action! *The Ultimates 2* #1 (February 2005), art by Bryan Hitch.

8

The Ultimates 2!

The Ultimates team of Millar, Hitch, and Neary reunited for a thirteen-issue sequel less than a year after the original series concluded.

In it, the media has learned the Ultimates' dark secret: The Hulk—who killed over 800 people in his rampage in New York City—is actually a member of the team. Nick Fury looks to control the damage, and it's decided that Banner will be put on trial for his crimes. He's defended by Daredevil's alter ego, Matt Murdock, but the evidence is overwhelming, and Banner is sentenced to death. Of course, it's not easy to kill the Hulk, so they drug Banner, and in his last assignment for the Ultimates, Hank Pym devises a way to execute him. But in the last page of the issue—a splash page—it's revealed that Pym secretly let him live. We see him from the back on a busy city street in an unidentified city. There are multiple flags hanging on poles outside of some of the buildings. None of them are the U.S. flag.

Where's Bruce Banner? *The Ultimates 2* #3 (April 2005), story by Mark Millar, art by Bryan Hitch and Paul Neary.

The sun is shining and there are palm trees in the background. This starts to give the reader some clues as to where Banner might be. In the bottom-right corner of the page, a man is reading a newspaper and we can partially see the headline. It says "El Hulk Ejecu …"

This is a clever bit of storytelling from Millar and Hitch. They don't give us a caption telling us where Banner has landed. There's no dialogue from him or any of the other people in the scene. There's just those visual clues and the newspaper—all there for an observant reader to discover and think about.

Real people continue to pop up as Janet and Betty go on the talk show circuit to defend the Ultimates. Speaking of Janet, she and Captain America are now a couple, as her soon-to-be ex-husband has further developed the technology that allows him to be Ant-Man. Iron Man and Black Widow have also hooked up, and Stark designs an Iron Widow suit for her—all black, of course. He asks her to marry him, and she accepts.

Millar's sense of humor is on display again when Captain America and Wasp walk down the street and discuss their lives. Captain America asks the Wasp, "Does this sixty-year age-gap thing ever get you down? I mean does it ever feel like you're dating Buck Rogers or something when we're having a conversation?" She, of course, responds, "Buck who?"

The scene ends with the pair about to be mugged by a group of men. That would normally lead to a five-page fight scene of

Great Britain's hero enters the story. *The Ultimates 2* #4 (May 2005), art by Bryan Hitch and Paul Neary.

Captain America and Wasp taking out their muggers, but here the action is all shown off-panel with only a word balloon from one of the bad guys that reads "urk!"

The team discovers Thor is actually a nurse who was suffering a mental breakdown when he stole cutting-edge technology from his brother—a harness that gives him super strength and the ability to fly and the mystical hammer, Mjolnir. Thor tells them they're being tricked by his brother Loki, the Asgardian God of Mischief.

The Ultimates are joined by Captain Britain, Captain Spain, Captain Italy, and Captain France—who doesn't wear an F on his forehead—to take the God of Thunder down. Thor beats all of them until Quicksilver rips off his harness, depriving him of his powers. They imprison him in the same cell that used to hold Banner.

Since he's kicked out of the Ultimates, Hank Pym joins The Defenders, a team that includes Nighthawk, Hellcat, The Valkyrie, Power Man, The Black Knight, and Son of Satan. While they're all based on characters from the regular Marvel universe, none of the Ultimate versions have any super-powers. They're essentially cosplayers who are calling themselves super heroes, but they don't have any real skills or experience. When Pym asks the Son of Satan if he's really Satan's son, he responds, "Are you on crack?"

This is an opportunity for Millar and Hitch to examine what

The Ultimates spend a lot of time fighting each other. This time it's Thor's turn. *The Ultimates 2* #5 (June 2005), story by Mark Millar, art by Bryan Hitch and Paul Neary.

would happen if normal people tried to become super heroes. The leader of the Defenders is Nighthawk, and he's excited for Pym to join the team because he has "eight more companies willing to sponsor us once we've got Giant Man on our books." Pym has to tell him that the Giant Man costume is owned by the U.S. government but he has a helmet that allows him to shrink and speak with ants.

After watching Pym shrink in size, Valkyrie says, "Man. Can you believe we've finally got somebody on the team with real super-powers?" We learn that Pym is using these well-meaning but hopelessly clueless people to try to get back into the Ultimates.

The Defenders are given a tip that a group of kids plan to steal cigarettes from a warehouse and they think that'll be an opportunity to get some good press. Things go terribly wrong when Nighthawk is soundly beaten by the teenagers and is only stopped from being burned alive when Pym grows into Giant Man. S.H.I.E.L.D. still had his Giant Man costume, so when he grows, his clothes are destroyed, and he's captured buck naked by a photographer for *The Daily Bugle*. The next day's newspaper has that photo accompanied by a headline that reads "Butt-er Luck Next Time."

So, the Defenders are played for laughs but it's also a commentary about hero worship and Pym's abuse of his position and power. It's also prescient about the world we live in today, where social media influencers are willing to do almost anything for fame and fortune.

Even though his time with the Defenders didn't work, Pym is still desperate to get back into Fury's good graces, and offers him two android war machines he's designed, Ultron and Vision Two. Not only does Fury turn him down, but Pym also learns that S.H.I.E.L.D. now has a platoon of Giant Men soldiers. And to make matters worse, they improved on his work, allowing the Giant Men to grow to 200 feet tall.

This story arc was collected in a trade paperback edition with the subtitle "Gods and Monsters!". The first issue was a hit, coming in as the second bestselling comic book of December 2004. The comic book ahead of it was another Avengers title, *The New Avengers* #1, written by Brian Michael Bendis.

The second story arc—titled "Grand Theft America!"—starts off with the Ultimates controversially taking out a nuclear facility in an unnamed Middle Eastern country and Hawkeye's wife and three kids being killed in a brutal home invasion that he's unable to stop. Hawkeye is kidnapped by his family's killers, and Captain America—who has just learned that Janet has been seeing her abusive ex-husband behind his back—is framed for their murders.

Between issues 7 and 8, *The Ultimates Annual* #1 was released. Written by Mark Millar with art by Steve Dillon, it tells the story of the Ultimates reserve team. Comprised of the Giant

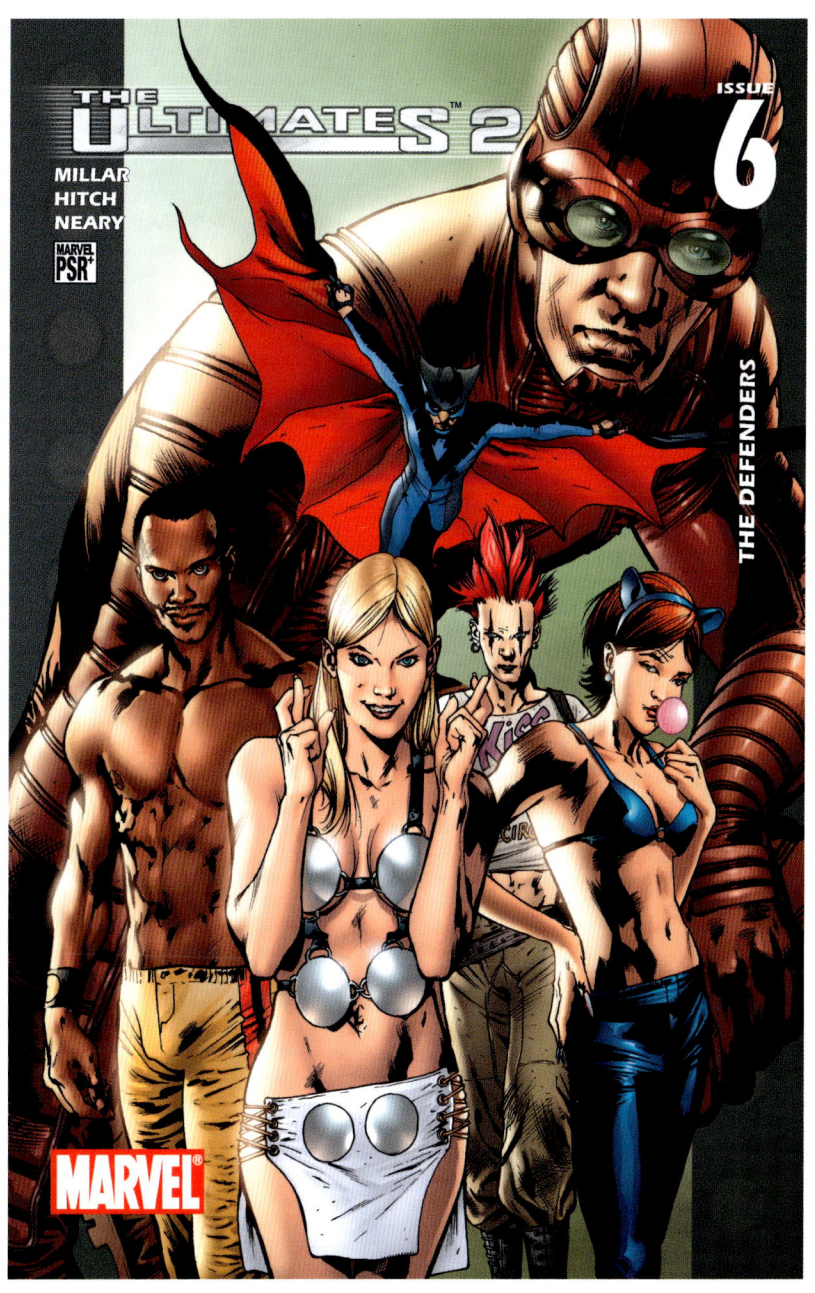

The Defenders! *The Ultimates 2* #6 (July 2005), art by Bryan Hitch and Paul Neary.

Men we've already seen, the reserve unit also includes three Rocketmen, who use a modified version of Iron Man's suit; and The Four Seasons, a group of Marines who are given suits that give them undefined powers.

Back in the main series, it's revealed that Hank Pym has been working with the Black Widow to betray the Ultimates and the United States. Super heroes from China (The Abomination and The Crimson Dynamo), Russia (Perun and The Schizoid Man), North Korea (Hurricane and Swarm), and an undefined Middle Eastern country (Captain Al-Rahman) have combined forces with Loki to conquer the United States. Millar introduces another unique twist by having our heroes battle villains from real-world countries. Outside of World War II-based comic books, when Marvel characters have problems around the world, it's usually in fictional countries like Latveria, Transia, Symkaria, and others.

As he's done with the classic Marvel super heroes who make up the Ultimates, Hitch's character design for these bad guys blends his realistic approach with the larger-than-life spectacle that comic books require. The designs look plausible—they're grounded with military- and country-specific details—but still recognizable as super villains. And, of course, they're villains to the U.S.-based heroes of the Ultimates but they're super heroes for the areas they represent.

Most of these characters have counterparts in the regular

The Giant Men in action. *The Ultimates 2 Annual* #1 (October 2005), story by Mark Millar, art by Steve Dillon.

Marvel universe, but Captain Al-Rahman is a new creation. His costume is designed to resemble the one Captain America wears. Where Captain America has a star on his chest, presumably to reflect that stars in the U.S. flag, Captain Al-Rahman has a W on his. Why a W? It's not explained. Instead of a shield, Captain Al-Rahman has a laser-type sword. He also got his powers through medical treatments similar to the ones Captain America underwent.

Millar is asking the reader to think about the idea of

The "Axis of Evil" bring their fight to the U.S. *The Ultimates 2* #10 (March 2006), story by Mark Millar, art by Bryan Hitch and Paul Neary.

American exceptionalism and the tit-for-tat nature of weapon development. If America has a patriotic super hero, why shouldn't other countries? Like Captain America, Captain Al-Rahman is an instrument of the government. Captain Al-Rahman doesn't believe the Ultimates should act as the world's protector. So, we have a story that's not the traditional super hero vs. super villain or good vs. evil type. Instead, it's a story about nation vs. nation, where each side believes they're doing the right thing.

These are smart comics. Millar and Hitch are telling a story that readers can think about after they've put an issue down.

In *The Ultimates 2*, these "bad guys" from the "axis of evil" call themselves The Liberators. With the help of Ultron androids provided by the treasonous Hank Pym, they easily take out the Ultimates reserve team and wreak havoc in every major U.S. city, including New York City where they topple the Statue of Liberty off her pedestal.

Where the first *The Ultimates* series had more scenes with the characters out of costume than ones where they were fighting, *The Ultimates 2* is more action-packed. This allows Hitch and Neary to showcase their storytelling skills. In the sequences that lead up to the destruction of the Statue of Liberty, Hitch's "rythym of storytelling" is again in play. There's a three-page multi-panel scene where we see The Triskelion destroyed. The art is extremely detailed and cinematically staged, so we feel like we're in the middle of the carnage. And, as he's done before, Millar steps aside and only has two small word balloons in the sequence.

That's followed a few pages later by a double-page spread where we see the Ultron androids smashing their way through a New York City street. The detail here is staggering, with dozens of the androids, eight massive skyscrapers, cars being overturned, and people fleeing. And, again, Millar doesn't use any text on these pages.

So, New York City is a mess, but the fight's not over. Stark takes out the Black Widow in a sequence that again emphasizes brains over brawn. The Black Widow is suddenly frozen in place. Stark tells her, "It's the nanites, darling. They're in your brain and your bloodstream and they allow you to control that armor I gave you … but guess who controls them?"

The other heroes fight back, and in a particularly gruesome scene, Hawkeye pulls out his fingernails so he can use them as weapons to kill the guards who are holding him captive. With help from the Wasp, Captain America also breaks free.

The battle moves to the White House, and as things look bad for our heroes, Banner returns and turns into the Hulk. But this time around, the Hulk appears to have some of the intellect of Banner, which allows him to more effectively help. The Ultimates are again joined by the super heroes from the European Union in what has now turned into a super hero

The Triskelion is brought down. *The Ultimates 2* #9 (January 2006), story by Mark Millar, art by Bryan Hitch and Paul Neary.

World War III. Things really start to turn The Ultimates' way when Janet Pym takes the Giant Man serum and Stark shows up in Iron Man Six, a spaceship-sized suit. The battle finally ends when Thor—who is revealed to be the God of Thunder he always said he was—takes out his half-brother Loki.

The battle scenes by Hitch and Neary throughout the last five issues are spectacular: action-packed storytelling with Hitch using his regular mix of double-page spreads and multi-panel pages. The double-page spreads create a cinematic, widescreen effect. The multi-panel pages often capture mid-motion action, ensuring the reader always knows where they are in the fight.

This is all done with a photorealistic, hyper-detailed style that allows for intense facial expressions and choreographed fights. The last issue comes with the largest comic book foldout

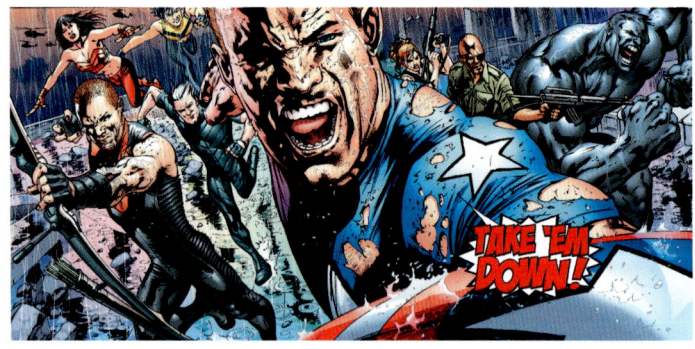

I guess Captain America didn't like "Avengers Assemble!" *The Ultimates 2* #13 (February 2007), story by Mark Millar, art by Bryan Hitch and Paul Neary.

I've ever seen—eight pages of a massive fight in front of the U.S. Capitol. If you like super hero comics, it doesn't get any better than this.

This extraordinary piece of comic book storytelling is the culmination of everything Mark Millar and Bryan Hitch have been building toward in this cinematic super hero story. It's the final showdown between the Ultimates and the bad guys, staged with an operatic sense of scale that pushes the widescreen comics they've been doing to a spread that's physically over four feet long. If you've only read this story digitally, you're missing the experience of spreading out this massive piece of art on your lap or a table. An experience that really lets you enter the story.

What makes this sequence so remarkable is not only the sheer amount of action packed into the pages, but also the way Hitch choreographs the battle so that every character is shown participating in a character-driven way. Captain America is taking on three aliens at once. The Hulk is smashing aliens all over the place. Quicksilver is seen in multiple places, using his speed to battle numerous aliens all at once.

And as we've seen many times in both *The Ultimates* and *The Ultimates 2*, Millar lets Hitch tell the story. There's no text on the eight-page spread.

The last page of the spread showcases Thor taking on his half-brother, Loki. In the pages that follow the giant spread,

Thor—likely still angry about having to endure doubts about his sanity–pummels Loki. Thor says, "You are filth! You are excrement! I refuse to fall before the shame of Asgard!"

And here's where Millar has another chance to show his talent. Loki could be just another angry bad guy who mindlessly wants to destroy the world. Instead, he has Loki say, "I was jealous, Thor. Jealous he [Odin] sent you to save the world. I only wanted you to fail so that he might smile on me for once." Now the reader has some empathy for the villain. It doesn't justify the horrible things he's done—particularly being complicit in the death of Hawkeye's family—but we can sympathize with him a bit.

As the series wraps up, Hawkeye—seeking revenge for the death of his family— assassinates Black Widow. In this scene, it's hard to have much sympathy for the Black Widow— the murder of Hawkeye's family is horrific and unjustifiable. She's done it for political reasons, calling Hawkeye "American trash,"

This is as good as super hero comics get. *The Ultimates 2* #13 (February 2007), story by Mark Millar, art by Bryan Hitch and Paul Neary.

and before he kills her, she taunts him by saying, "Got a message for the wife and kids, Hawkeye? Anything you'd like me to pass along?" He responds by saying, "You won't see them where you're going, comrade."

This is a brutal scene and while it's not explicitly discussed, Hawkeye is acting as judge and executioner. Black Widow has wronged him in the most vicious way possible, but does Hawkeye have the right to assassinate her? This is heady stuff for a super hero comic. Millar is working at the top of his game and this thought-provoking story is a testament to his skill.

The final twist is when the Ultimates decide to stop working for the U.S. government, and Stark agrees to independently finance them. Stark explains that "removing our super-soldiers from state control leaves the President free to sign this superhuman test ban treaty Russia and China have been pushing for." So, as the story comes to an end, Millar again uses the super hero universe as a metaphor for the real one the reader lives in.

Black Widow pays the ultimate price for her betrayal of Hawkeye and the team. *The Ultimates 2* #13 (February 2007), story by Mark Millar, art by Bryan Hitch and Paul Neary.

In a four-page epilogue, the action flashes back to 1942 in a gentle scene where Steve Rogers is on his date with his fiancée, Gail. Rogers is about to ship out to fight in World War II and Gail asks him if he's scared. A hero through and through, he says, "Nah, I want this more than I've ever wanted anything. I've wanted to fight the krauts since I saw my first newsreel." The scene ends with a splash page of them sharing a romantic kiss in front of the classic World War II recruitment poster that shows Uncle Sam pointing his finger at the viewer and saying "I Want You for the U.S. Army."

The only text on the page is: "The Ultimates Volumes One and Two Dedicated with Love to Stan and Jack."

The story comes to an end. *The Ultimates 2* #13 (February 2007), story by Mark Millar, art by Bryan Hitch and Paul Neary.

9

Where Are They Now?

Paul Neary

Millar, Hitch, and Neary worked together again in 2008 on a high-profile *Fantastic Four* run titled "World's Greatest." Their first issue was released in April 2008, just nine months after the last issue of *The Ultimates 2*. Neary inked the first two issues (Nos. 554 and 555), with Currie taking over with #556.

In addition to the two issues of *Fantastic Four*, Neary also inked a number of Hitch's covers for Marvel. Titles they worked on together included *Ultimate Doom*, *Captain America: Man Out of Time*, *Wolverine: Best There Is*, *Age of Ultron*, and others.

Paul Neary passed away on February 10, 2024. He was 74 years old.

The *Ultimates* creative team reunited on the *Fantastic Four*. *Fantastic Four* #554 (April 2008). Art by Bryan Hitch.

Andrew Currie

As just mentioned, Currie reunited with Millar and Hitch on the same *Fantastic Four* run that Neary started. Hitch and Currie also worked together in 2021 on the first sixteen issues of *Venom*. In 2023, they worked together on the four-issue series *Ultimate Invasion*, written by Jonathan Hickman. This title kicked off the 2023 Ultimate Universe relaunch we'll discuss shortly. Currie is currently inking the covers for Bryan Hitch's creator-owned comic series.

Bryan Hitch

Hitch continues to be a popular comic book artist—a fan favorite appreciated for the unique approach he takes to storytelling and for his exciting covers. As already mentioned, he continued to work with all of his *Ultimates* collaborators.

After working on many high-profile non-Marvel super hero titles, Hitch is currently working with Geoff Johns on a creator-owned series.

Mark Millar

After finishing his work on *The Ultimates*, Millar has gone on to become one of the most successful comic book writers of all time.

As *The Ultimates 2* was wrapping up, he started writing an influential run on *Wolverine* and launched the Ultimate version of Fantastic Four, co-writing the first six issues of the series with Brian Michael Bendis. Millar would return to *Ultimate Fantastic Four* on issue #21, with a story that introduced

Mark Millar takes the Marvel Universe to Civil War. *Civil War* #1 (July 2006). Art by Steve McNiven.

the concept of an alternate Earth inhabited by Marvel Zombies.

The biggest Marvel title Millar worked on after *The Ultimates* was 2006's seven-issue *Civil War* mini-series. Drawn by Steve McNiven, this massive event involved all of Marvel's major characters and crossed over into dozens of titles. The high concept is a good one: after another devastating superpower fight led to disaster, the U.S. government passed the Super Hero Registration Act, which required super heroes to provide the government with their real names. Captain America led the heroes opposed to the Act, and Iron Man led those in favor of it. This story builds on the themes Millar explored in *The Ultimates* around government regulation of super heroes and can also be seen as a further exploration of the security-conscious real world that continued to develop after the 9/11 terrorist attacks. The series was used as the inspiration for the 2016 movie *Captain America: Civil War*.

In 2007, Millar returned to *Wolverine* for another important run drawn by his *Civil War* partner, Steve McNiven. "Old Man Logan" takes place in an alternate future universe where the super heroes have lost to the supervillains. The Red Skull is president, and other supervillains control vast territories of the U.S. Logan—Wolverine's real name—is forced out of retirement when he needs money to pay his evil landlords— the grandchildren of the Hulk. This story was one of the

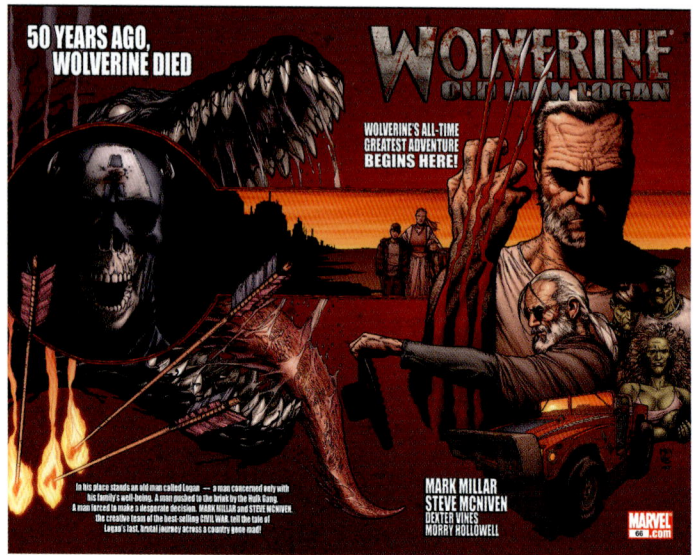

The "Old Man Logan" story starts here. *Wolverine* #66 (August 2008), art by Steve McNiven and Dexter Vines.

inspirations for the 2017 movie *Logan*, and this version of the character also appeared in the 2024 movie *Deadpool & Wolverine*.

As previously discussed, 2008 saw Millar reunited with Hitch on a *Fantastic Four* run. That year was also when *Marvel 1985* was released. This nostalgic look back at the comics of the 1980s was drawn by Tommy Lee Edwards.

In addition to his Marvel work, Millar launched Millarworld, his own shared fictional universe, in 2003. Initially publishing titles through a variety of companies, *Kick-Ass* was released in 2008 by Marvel through its short-lived creator-owned imprint,

Icon. With art by John Romita, Jr., *Kick-Ass* tells the story of a teenage boy—with no super-powers—who decides to put on a costume and fight crime. The series was popular and led to a number of comic book sequels and two movies: 2010's *Kick-Ass* and 2013's *Kick-Ass 2*.

In 2009, Millar returned to *The Ultimates* characters in *The Ultimate Avengers*. Published over eighteen issues, with three different artists, Millar adds new characters to the team, including Punisher and Blade. That series led to 2011's *Ultimate Avengers vs. New Ultimates*, part of a "Death of Spider-Man" story that was also being told in *Ultimate Spider-Man*. When Peter Parker nobly dies in this story, Miles Morales—who was also bitten by a genetically modified spider—becomes Spider-Man.

In 2012, Millar was awarded an honorary doctorate for literature from Glasgow Caledonian University. In 2013, he received an MBE from the Queen for his services to film and literature.

The Ultimates

The Ultimates characters continued to have their stories told by other creators. The previously mentioned *Ultimate Avengers vs. New Ultimates*—which was written by Millar and was part

Mark Millar's last work in the Ultimate universe. *Ultimate Avengers vs. New Avengers* #6 (September 2011), art by Leinil Francis Yu.

of a relaunch known as Ultimate Comics Universe Reborn—concluded in the summer of 2011. Later that year, a new ongoing series was launched and given the somewhat confusing title *Ultimate Comics: The Ultimates*. This series was initially written by Jonathan Hickman with art by Esad Ribic. The other titles in the Ultimate line were also relaunched as *Ultimate Comics: Spider-Man* and *Ultimate Comics: X-Men*.

Ultimate Comics: The Ultimates would run for thirty issues and end as part of the "Cataclysm" story that involved the characters from all of the Ultimate titles. In this story, Galactus is sent from the main Marvel universe into the Ultimate one. This isn't the Gah Lak Tus we've already discussed; the one from the Marvel universe is even tougher. *The Ultimates* part of the story was told in a three-issue series called *Cataclysm: Ultimate Comics Ultimates*, written by Joshua Hale Fialkov with art by Carmine Di Giandomenico and Lorenzo Ruggiero; and a five-issue series called *Cataclysm: The Ultimates' Last Stand*, written by Brian Michael Bendis with art by Mark Bagley and Andrew Hennessy. I think it's safe to say that, by this time, these comics had strayed far off the path of being accessible for new readers.

After the events of "Cataclysm," the Ultimates team decided to call it quits, and a new team was formed, with their adventures being told in *All-New Ultimates*. This series ran for twelve issues and was written by Michel Fiffe with art by Amilcar Pinna and others. The new team included Spider-Man,

Black Widow, Kitty Pryde, Bombshell, and Cloak and Dagger. Rather than take on global threats, they focused on crimes in the Hell's Kitchen area of New York City.

In 2015, Marvel brought back their company-wide crossover event *Secret Wars*. The first *Secret Wars* came out in 1984 and was so successful it set the template that would be used for all "event" stories going forward. The main story is told in a finite series, with many of the company's individual titles telling other parts of the story. The 2015 version comprised nine issues and was written by Jonathan Hickman with art by Esad Ribic. The premise is that all of the alternate Marvel Earths are destroyed and replaced by a Battleworld. This allowed for alternate versions of the same characters to appear in the story. It's also where the stories about the Ultimate versions of the characters would stop—in the aptly named *Ultimate End*, a five-issue series written by Brian Michael Bendis with art by Mark Bagley and Scott Hanna.

A new Ultimates team—with characters and stories from the now consolidated Marvel universe—was launched out of *Secret Wars*. There were twelve issues of *The Ultimates* and ten issues of *The Ultimates 2*. These stories were written by Al Ewing working with a number of artists. This version of the team included Black Panther, Ms. America, Captain Marvel, Blue Marvel, and Spectrum, and they went back to dealing with global problems. In a nice touch, Marvel numbered the last issue of *The Ultimates 2*—which came out in 2016—as #100. And, with that, *The Ultimates* would come to an end.

Just kidding! Stories never end in comics!

In 2023, Marvel brought back the Ultimate Universe in *Ultimate Invasion*, a four-issue series written by Jonathan Hickman with art by—surprise!—Hitch and Currie. Bringing back two of the original creators for this relaunch was a great idea by Marvel's editorial team, but this version of the Ultimate Universe is completely different to the one that preceded it. It's not necessarily intended for new readers and is a more radical reimagining of the characters. As of this writing, titles in the line include *Ultimate Spider-Man*, *Ultimate Black Panther*, *Ultimate X-Men*, *Ultimate Wolverine*, and, of course, *The Ultimates*.

10

The Ultimates Shape Pop Culture!

Millar and Hitch's take on Marvel's classic super hero team immediately resonated with comic book readers of the early 2000s. Their relaunch reimagined the origins of some of Marvel's most popular characters, establishing them for a twenty-first-century audience. These heroes were recognized as celebrities, often mingling with real-world entertainers and politicians. They were also part of the answer to the question of how super hero stories could be told in a post-9/11 world.

In the real world, after the 9/11 terrorist attacks, the U.S. quickly created the Transportation Security Administration (TSA), forever changing how U.S. citizens would pass through airports. The Department of Homeland Security (DHS) was then established, consolidating twenty-two federal agencies into a single department that would coordinate efforts on stopping terrorist attacks.

After Magneto's attack on Washington, D.C., the U.S. government funds the Ultimates. While never directly addressing 9/11, anyone reading *The Ultimates* in the early 2000s would be thinking that this might be the way the U.S. would respond if super heroes were real.

The Marvel universe has always taken place in the real world—the action happens in New York City, not a fictional city like Metropolis—and *The Ultimates* carries that tradition forward. It's this combination of real-world people and events combined with fictional characters and situations that makes these powerful and fantastic stories resonate with audiences.

In the world of comic books, Hitch's widescreen art—with big panels and hyper-realistic detail and violence— has influenced the generation of comic book artists who have followed him. Millar's fast-paced plots, witty dialogue, and well-developed characters have done the same for comic book writers. The comics have been so successful and read by so many, it's impossible to overstate their impact on readers and creators alike.

And, of course, the comics remain in print. The most recent collected edition is 2022's *The Ultimates Omnibus*—the third edition of the book that gathers together all of Millar and Hitch's work in a single 880-page hardcover volume. New readers and creators are experiencing the work for the first time every day. How it will influence them will be fun to learn.

NOTES

1. Eric Reynolds, "Industry Sales Records in 1993 Shadowed by Collapse of Speculator Boom," *Comics Journal* #166, February 1994, p. 27.

2. Jason Sacks and Keith Dallas, *American Comic Book Chronicles: 1990s*, 1st edn. (Raleigh: TwoMorrows, 2018), p. 279.

3. "An Oral History of Marvel Knights," https://www.marvel.com/oral-history-marvel-knights.

4. Brian Michael Bendis, "Ramblings," *Ultimate Spider-Man Omnibus*, 1st edn. (New York: Marvel, 2012), p. 879.

5. "Mark Bagley Interview," September 15, 2000, https://www.cbr.com/mark-bagley-interview/.

6. Sean Howe, *Marvel Comics: The Untold Story*, 1st edn. (New York: HarperCollins, 2012), p. 405.

7. Christian Holub, "Mark Millar on his new Netflix comic *The Magic Order* and the origins of the MCU," *Entertainment Weekly*, April 6, 2018, https://ew.com/books/2018/04/06/mark-millar-on-his-new-netflix-comic-the-magic-order-and-the-origins-of-the-mcu/.

8. Tony Isabella, "Ultimately—Good, Bad, and Ugly?" *Comics Buyer's Guide* #1515, November 29, 2002, p. 18.

9. John Rhett Thomas, "The Spotlight Interview with Mark Millar," *Marvel Spotlight: Mark Millar/Steve McNiven*, 2006, p. 19.

10. Jack Abramowitz, "Reading Room," *Comics Buyer's Guide* #1515, November 29, 2002, p. 23.

11 Ron Richards, "Ultimate Comics Universe Reborn With The Ultimates #1 By Jonathan Hickman and Esad Ribic," *iFanboy*, May 2, 2011, https://ifanboy.com/articles/ultimate-comics-universe-reborn-with-the-ultimates-1-by-jonathan-hickman-and-esad-ribic/.

ACKNOWLEDGMENTS

I've had a long career publishing comic books and had the good fortune to have many mentors. Dean Mullaney, Jan Mullaney, and cat yronwode gave me my first comics job at Eclipse Comics in 1990 and I'd likely have a boring job in finance if it wasn't for them. Mike Richardson, Jim Lee, John Nee, Todd McFarlane, and Terry Fitzgerald also employed me throughout the 1990s and I learned most of what I know about publishing from them.

In 1999, I started IDW Publishing with three friends—Robbie Robbins, Alex Garner, and Kris Oprisko. Together we built a company that has—unbelievably—recently celebrated its twenty-fifth anniversary. At IDW, I had the good fortune to work with a number of people who helped IDW grow and that I'm proud to know as friends—Greg Goldstein, Matt Ruzicka, Chris Ryall, Scott Dunbier, Lorelei Bunjes, Dirk Wood, Kevin Eastman, Allison Baker, Justin Eisinger, Alonzo Simon, Mike Ford, Joe Hill, Jeff Webber, Steve Niles, Rick Privman, Yumiko Miyano, Gabe Rodriguez, Tom Waltz, and many, many others.

After leaving IDW, my best bud, Robbie, and I decided to

start another company, Clover Press, with Nate Murray and Elaine La Rosa. Matt Ruzicka and Hank Kanalz came on board when I decided to retire and, along with Zac Boone and Kurtis Findlay, they continue to publish books that make me proud.

Beau Smith and Chris Pitzer, fellow Eclipse Comics alums, are as good friends as one could have. They always brighten my day.

John Jackson Miller's comichron.com provided the sales data I used in this book, and Grand Comics Database at comics.org provided the release dates. Both sites are invaluable to anyone writing about or researching comic books.

Gareb Shamus, Jim McLauchlin, and all the writers and editors at *Wizard* who interviewed comics creators in the 1990s and early 2000s produced a treasure chest of primary source material for a book like this one.

I've been teaching a class at Portland State University about publishing comic books and the enthusiasm I've seen from the students who've taken it makes me optimistic about the medium's future. I appreciate Diana Schutz and Susan Kirtley inviting me to join them at PSU.

Thanks to University Library Dean Scott Walter and Comic Arts Librarian Pamela Jackson, San Diego State University is the home of the Ted Adams and Robbie Robbins IDW Founders Collection, which includes more than 20,000 IDW titles. Other friends at SDSU who helped shepherd our collection are Professor Elizabeth Pollard, Karena Sara, and Michelle LaGrandeur.

I wouldn't be writing this book if it wasn't for Sven Larsen at Marvel and Haaris Naqvi, Leah Babb-Rosenfeld, and Hali Han at Bloomsbury. Thanks for giving me the opportunity.

This book—obviously—wouldn't have been possible without the work of Mark Millar, Bryan Hitch, Andrew Currie, and Paul Neary. Thanks for creating comics that have stood the test of time.

My in-laws, Ed and Cindy, have always shown me kindness and love. I also gained two brothers when I married. Christian, who has no interest in comics, and Mark, who shares my passions for them.

My mom and dad encouraged me to read and supported my comic book hobby when I was growing up. Every family vacation included trips to the local comic book shop and used bookstores. The support and love they always showed me gave me every opportunity to chase my dreams.

My sister, Jenny, who had to suffer through all those store visits, has always been there for me.

My son, Sam, is a kind and smart man. I'm proud of you.

My wife, Paula, brings happiness and joy to my life every day. I love you.

ILLUSTRATIONS

The Avengers #1 cover. Credit: Jack Kirby and Dick Ayers.	4
The Incredible Hulk #377 cover. Credit: Dale Keown and Bob McLeod.	11
Fantastic Four #1 cover. Credit: Jim Lee and Scott Williams.	14
Ultimate Spider-Man #1 cover. Credit Joe Quesada.	27
Ultimate X-Men #1, pages 17–18. Credit: Adam Kubert and Art Thibert.	31
Captain America Comics #1, page 5. Credit: Joe Simon and Jack Kirby.	43
The Ultimates #1, cover. Credit: Bryan Hitch and Andrew Currie.	46
The Ultimates #1, pages 6–7. Credit: Bryan Hitch and Andrew Currie.	48
The Ultimates No 1, page 14. Credit: Bryan Hitch and Andrew Currie.	50
The Ultimates No 2, page 3, panel 1. Credit: Bryan Hitch and Andrew Currie.	51
Ultimate Marvel Team-Up #4, cover. Credit: Mike Allred.	53

The Ultimates No 3, pages 18–19. Credit: Bryan Hitch and Andrew Currie.	56
The Avengers #16, page 11, panel 1. Credit: Jack Kirby and Dick Ayers.	58
The Ultimates #4, page 22. Credit: Bryan Hitch and Andrew Currie.	60
The Ultimates #5, pages 3–4. Credit: Bryan Hitch and Andrew Currie.	62
The Ultimates #6, page 17. Credit: Bryan Hitch and Andrew Currie.	66
The Ultimates #5, page 14. Credit: Bryan Hitch and Andrew Currie.	69
The Ultimates #7, page 1. Credit: Bryan Hitch and Andrew Currie.	70
The Ultimates #7, cover. Credit: Bryan Hitch and Andrew Currie.	73
Amazing Adventures #1, cover. Credit: Jack Kirby and John Romita	77
The Ultimates #8, page 14. Credit: Bryan Hitch and Paul Neary.	79
The Ultimates #9, page 9. Credit: Bryan Hitch and Paul Neary.	82
The Ultimates #10, page 3. Credit: Bryan Hitch and Paul Neary.	85

ILLUSTRATIONS

The Ultimates #10, page 4. Credit: Bryan Hitch and Paul Neary.	87
The Ultimates #10, pages 10–11. Credit: Bryan Hitch and Paul Neary.	88
The Ultimates #10, page 21. Credit: Bryan Hitch and Paul Neary.	90
The Ultimates #11, page 1. Credit: Bryan Hitch and Paul Neary.	93
The Ultimates #12, page 24. Credit: Bryan Hitch and Paul Neary.	97
The Ultimates #13, page 9, panel 3. Credit: Bryan Hitch and Paul Neary.	100
Ultimate Nightmare #1, cover. Credit: Trevor Hairsine.	104
Ultimate Nightmare #2, page 3, panel 1. Credit: Trevor Hairsine, Nelson DeCastro, and Simon Coleby.	106
The Ultimates 2 #1, cover. Credit: Bryan Hitch.	108
The Ultimates 2 #3, page 23. Credit: Bryan Hitch and Paul Neary.	110
The Ultimates 2 #4, cover. Credit: Bryan Hitch and Paul Neary.	112
The Ultimates 2 #5, page 2. Credit: Bryan Hitch and Paul Neary.	114
The Ultimates 2 #6, cover. Credit: Bryan Hitch and Paul Neary.	117

The Ultimates 2 Annual #1, page 22. Credit: Steve Dillon.	119
The Ultimates 2 #10, page 5, panel 3. Credit: Bryan Hitch and Paul Neary.	120
The Ultimates 2 #9, page 6. Credit: Bryan Hitch and Paul Neary.	123
The Ultimates 2 #13, pages 12–13, panel 3. Credit: Bryan Hitch and Paul Neary.	124
The Ultimates 2 #13, eight-page gatefold spread. Credit: Bryan Hitch and Paul Neary.	126
The Ultimates 2 #13, page 36. Credit: Bryan Hitch and Paul Neary.	128
The Ultimates 2 #13, page 45. Credit: Bryan Hitch and Paul Neary.	130
Fantastic Four #554, direct market cover. Credit: Bryan Hitch.	132
Civil War #1, cover. Credit: Steve McNiven.	134
Wolverine #66, cover. Credit: Steve McNiven and Dexter Vines.	136
Ultimate Avengers vs. New Avengers #6, Cover. Credit: Leinil Francis Yu.	138

ABOUT THE AUTHOR

Ted Adams has spent thirty-five years in publishing, initially working for a variety of companies, including Eclipse Comics, Dark Horse, Jim Lee's WildStorm, and Todd McFarlane Productions. In 1999, he co-founded IDW Publishing and was that company's CEO and Publisher for 20 years, negotiating deals to publish *Transformers*, *Teenage Mutant Ninja Turtles*, *Star Trek*, and many more licensed and creator-owned titles. Under his leadership, the company won dozens of industry awards, including many Eisner and Harvey Awards. He's proud to have been the publisher of a line of Marvel comics aimed at kids and the prestigious Artist's Edition line, which included many classic Marvel titles. IDW purchased Top Shelf in 2015, and he helped expand the reach of their titles, including John Lewis's *March* trilogy. *March Book Three* won the National Book Award for Young People's Literature in 2016.

As CEO, he helped take IDW public and used some of the proceeds to finance TV shows including *Locke & Key*, *Dirk Gently*, and *Wynonna Earp*. He's an executive producer on those and other TV shows and films.

After leaving IDW in 2018, he co-founded Clover Press with his long-time business partner, Robbie Robbins. Now mostly retired, he volunteers for several non-profit organizations, which have included the Comic Book Legal Defense Fund, San Diego's Traveling Stories, and Southern Oregon University's Foundation Board of Trustees. He has taught a class on comics publishing for Portland State University and has an MBA from the University of Notre Dame. He is the recipient of Southern Oregon University's Distinguished Alumni Award.

Adams has also written comic books and graphic novels, including an adaptation of *The Great Gatsby*.

MARVEL AGE OF COMICS

Explore the series!

www.bloomsbury.com/marvel-books

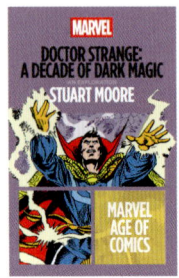

Doctor Strange: A Decade of Dark Magic
by Stuart Moore

The story of one of Marvel's most bizarre, otherworldly heroes, beginning with his creation at the hands of Stan Lee and artist/plotter Steve Ditko, and discussed against the backdrop of one of the most turbulent decades in American history.

Daredevil: Born Again
by Chris Ryall

A smart, meticulous look into the compelling and original storyline of *Daredevil: Born Again*, its gorgeous and unique artwork, and its overall influence in the decades since its release.

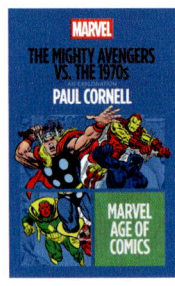

The Mighty Avengers vs. the 1970s
by Paul Cornell

The Avengers was **the** comic book of the 1970s. From Civil Rights to Women's Lib, battles for the soul of America became battles between super heroes.

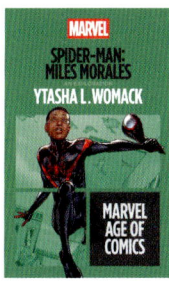

Spider-Man: Miles Morales
by Ytasha L. Womack

A look at the hugely successful reimagining of one of the most popular super hero characters of all time.

Wolverine: Weapon X
by Jim Rugg

A deep-dive into one of Marvel's most experimental and brutal comics, and what many consider to be **the** definitive Wolverine story.